When you are dead

Seek for your resting place

Not in the earth

But in the hearts of men.

- Rumi

A catalogue record for this work is available from the National Library of Australia

Hartley, Simon (author)
The Devil Thumbs A Ride
ISBN: 978-1-9227227-2-0
AUTOBIOGRAPHY

Typeset Calluna Regular 10/17

Cover and book design by Green Hill Publishing

A biography of transgression and hope

THE DEVIL
THUMBS A RIDE

SIMON HARTLEY

CONTENTS

PROLOGUE

We had just arrived in Denpasar for a ten-day Balinese holiday. I was with a young and beautiful girlfriend. We walked through the airport terminal and joined the queue for customs. No-one knew that I had smuggled a substantial amount of heroin and methadone onto the plane and was now carrying it through the airport. After waiting in the queue for just a couple of minutes, I noticed an Indonesian policeman looking at me. As I looked away, I realised that he had started walking towards me, and he had a sniffer dog. All I had was a few seconds to think of something, anything. Perhaps a distraction of some kind... and it was going to have to be a bloody good one.

I stepped out of the line.

THE ROAD TO LOVE

Tonight, I spy a gentle friend
On a road to love that never ends
Hiding in a secret dream
A soft embrace that's never been

Now I'm all alone
I turn and head for home
All but life has left me
It's down this road I go
I walk this path alone
With nothing but the wind behind me

From the smallest seed to the tallest tree
A shower of rain on the darkest sea
The brightest star lighting up the dark
A glimpse of dust into human love

I keep looking for a place
That never comes my way
The lovers I have lost, I think about the cost
And all the souls that touched me

As Lazarus would say
There has to be a way
Regrets and lies we carry
I hope I've given back
Not fallen in a trap
With clowns, thieves, and mad men
Cruel is the pain of sad men
Only fools say the end with Amen

Tonight, I spy a gentle friend
On a road to love that never ends
Hiding in a secret dream
A soft embrace that's never been

Chapter One

ENGLAND

In the moon tides memory sing me a deeper song

I have been living in Australia for forty-six years. I was born in Lancashire on the 12th of February 1963, the coldest month in the coldest year ever recorded in England. The famous poet, Sylvia Plath, had taken her own life the day before, and the Young family, soon to leave for Australia and go on to conquer the world as AC/DC, were buried in eight feet of snow in Scotland.

My family had no reason to be so far north except for my father's work. We moved to Cheshire about a year later, again for Dad's work. We had no relatives in either place but settled in Knutsford, a small town founded a thousand years earlier by a Danish king called Knut, better known as King Canute. I had three siblings. Liz was the firstborn. Andrew, the first son, was destined for a great tragedy. I was the middle child and Chris was the youngest by a year. All very nice and Christian, or so I thought. I was a happy-go-lucky kid, quite tall and strong, with blue eyes and fair, almost white hair.

My father, was already on his way to a successful career in the textile industry and at the same time was proving to be a sailing champion, and went on to win the British titles in 1975. He was still quite young, handsome and charming. He was also very business savvy and, to my mother's detriment, a womaniser. His mother had left my grandfather and taken Dad away when he was just a boy. I have never believed the official explanation for why this happened. I do know my father never saw his father again, ever! I understand now just how big an impact that must have had on Dad, and I believe it stayed with him until the end. So, Dad had no father, he was an only child, and to my grandma, he was the blond-haired, blue-eyed golden boy. My brothers and sister grew up in awe of him. I thought he was okay, and I was certainly not his favourite, which my mum tried to make up for. I did love him, though. He was my dad.

My mother had a very different start in life to my father. Mum was born into abject poverty a few years before the war, with an older and younger brother, a weak, vulnerable mother, and an abusive and alcoholic father. He dodged the war effort and was known in the neighbourhood as a coward. There was barely any food, and they were never going to be sent to the countryside during the war, as my father was.

My grandfather on Mum's side was an alcoholic. He abused his wife, beat his children, and sexually abused my mother.

He was never held to account. The last time I saw him, I was fifteen. He had just had a leg amputated and was about to have his other leg sawn off, probably from a lifetime of doing nothing but heavy smoking and drinking. I didn't know at the time what he had done and what he was. I wish I had. To this day I have a clear memory of him sitting there watching television, with one leg missing, and knowing he was about to lose the other; tragic, pathetic, and perhaps even evil!

Mum was rescued by the headmistress of her school and spent the rest of her childhood away from her family. My mum was a dedicated and kind mother. She was very community-minded and was always helping others, which included fostering some pretty messed-up kids. Her past abuse at the hands of her father eventually caught up with her after we had emigrated to Australia, when the family was torn apart by Dad's ambition and infidelity.

As a young boy, I saw Mum save a man's life in Malta on a family holiday. He had cut an artery on a jagged broken tile and, if not for Mum, he would have died. He had lost a huge amount of blood and was slipping away in front of his children when we arrived, and Mum took over from a group who were panicking and just did not know what they were doing. Mum stopped the bleeding until the paramedics arrived. She saved a boy's life in another incident at a pool when he knocked himself out in the water and needed resuscitating. I was with Mum when I saw my best friend's cousin drown, and I watched Mum fight for half an hour to bring him back, as the ambulance was slow to arrive. I stood next to his brother and watched him die.

For me, growing up in the '60s and '70s, in a small country town in Cheshire with its lakes and woods, was wonderful. I was close to my brothers, and I had a large, diverse group of friends. We sailed racing dinghies every weekend on a picturesque lake at Budworth, not ten miles away, and we often travelled the country competing in national competitions. We were all natural sailors, except for my mother, but she nearly always came with us. We won competitions that were well-attended by sailors from around the country. At age twelve, I sailed in the under-eighteens world championship in Trieste, Italy. I finished in second place, with over sixteen countries represented and about five to seven boats from each country. It was 1975, one year before I moved to the other side of the world. My accommodation in the beautiful seaside town of Trieste was a university dorm, and I can still remember coming down the stairs for breakfast and smelling real coffee for the first time.

Dad's career was taking off, and we moved into a two-hundred-dred-year-old coach house on a beautiful street called Leah Road. It had been made into a lovely home with a large garden that led down to a small, wooded area, a river, and some small lakes, perfect for exploring on homemade rafts with my brothers and friends. It was an adventure playground.

We spent years building bridges, digging tunnels, and declaring war on anyone who just happened to come by. We had catapults, bows and arrows, and even an air rifle, not to mention all sorts of pits and booby traps. God knows why, but my parents bought Andrew an air rifle. He wasn't exactly a saint - his middle name should have been Mischief, and he took delight in being bad.

He was great at justifying some of his antics by saying, "Come on, what's the worst that can happen?"

I'd reply with, "Well, Mum and Dad will kill us for a start."

"Ah, yes," he would say with a rather large dose of sarcasm, "but will they, really?"

He would go on to explain in a very logical way all the potential punishments we might receive. You know the sort of things: we might be grounded for a week and/or spanked, locked in our rooms, or be allowed no television for a week. No matter the punishment, it would, in Andrew's opinion, be well worth it. Chris and I would usually agree and off we would go. He was the big brother, after all. One summer's day we were in a great hiding spot in the woods, camouflaged and lying down like snipers.

"What are we doing now?" I asked.

"We," Andrew turned to look at me with his serious face, "are being quiet."

We saw some people from the village on horses, in their fine riding clothes. It appeared to us as if they were very much in uniform and that must mean they were the enemy. I'm not sure why that meant they were the enemy, but the important thing was that it got the adrenaline going.

Andrew looked at us and said, "Right, no-one make's a sound, then we run for it."

Before we could ask what he was going to do, he shot the horse in the buttock. It made a fair old crack, and the horse bucked, whinnied, and took off like a wild beast, the poor rider hanging on for dear life and the other riders chasing after her. We ran for our lives.

Every weekday, my brothers and sister headed off to grammar school by bus, while I walked a few miles in another direction to a comprehensive school. I presume now that my grades were too low for a private education. There was a lot of fighting at my school, and I was usually in the thick of it. It was well attended by the kids from the Long Ridge housing estate and many of them were very poor and aggressive. They presumed they could bully, harass, and intimidate my friends and me. Well, I wasn't having that and the only thing that seemed to work was fighting back. It's not that I wanted to fight, but if you didn't back down, there would be a fight. I learned boxing at school and judo after school. I would get embroiled in a fight every week or so. It got so bad with one boy, who was the school bully, that the headmaster called us into his office and told us he had organised a fight in the boxing ring. Five rounds in front of the whole school. There were two and a half thousand kids at my school, so it got attention and there was a lot on the line. I took it very seriously and trained every day for hours with my brothers and friends. Fight day arrived and Chris and I went at each other as hard as we could. He was like a wild animal, but I kept my cool, ducking and weaving, jabbing, and punching, until I landed a right hook to the head, and he went down in the second round. I broke his nose in the third round, and as his blood gushed, the headmaster called an end to the fight. The whole school went crazy! The funny thing was, it worked, and we became friends. I think that's what boys do. Or rather, that's what they used to do.

I was in middle school when mum took me to a small local hospital to get a mole removed from my belly button, which didn't seem like a big deal at the time. I arrived at the hospital and before I knew what was happening, I was on the operating table breathing in the gas. I remember counting down, "Ten, nine, eight, seven, six, five, four...", and then nothing. I must have gone deep because the next thing I remember, I was looking up at the wrong end of a long, dark tunnel with a very faint light that appeared to be way off in the distance. No matter how hard I tried, I just could not reach the light. I wanted to wake up but couldn't. I was trapped and it was scary as hell. I thought I had been buried alive. I had no recollection of the operation or even being in hospital. I was sinking deeper and deeper into a dark abyss, and it felt as though I was between life and oblivion.

I was told the next day that I had been struggling and thrashing about, and I kicked one of the nurses in the face, breaking her glasses. I supposed that at least they would stop calling her four eyes! It took another two nurses and a doctor to come in and hold me down, while I called out for Mum. I think that experience had a profound impact, deep down in my soul. It was the stuff of nightmares. Apart from that, and the time the neighbour's weird teenager split my head open with an iron spear, it was generally a good time to be a kid, and life was filled with adventure.

I had no idea then, but my father's affairs had been going on for some time. Mum was starting to show signs of sadness and stress, and her behaviour had started to become a little erratic. I walked into my parents' bedroom late one night after hearing some scary noises, and I saw Dad and my sister Liz holding Mum. They were trying to calm her down while she vomited up pills. I stood in the doorway crying. It was the saddest sight. I was scared, and I needed Mum to be okay. That night I witnessed how brave and amazing my sister was.

Apparently, we were going to emigrate to Australia. How did I know this? Well, I was informed by a family friend, who told me Dad had been offered a promotion. I mentioned it to my friends at school and they all fell about laughing. I laughed with them, as I didn't believe it either. I can't remember talking about it as a family at all, but within a few short weeks we were on a plane. We stopped in Mauritius for a week's holiday, as it seemed the whole family needed a severe case of sunstroke! We arrived on Australian soil in January 1976. I turned thirteen a month later.

One needs to pay in advance

Embrace grief with heavy cost

For in wisdom

Is much suffering

Increase your knowledge

You increase your sorrow

This is a fleeting world

Which in some strange way

Keeps calling us

Pulling our eyes

Heavenward

Chapter Two

AUSTRALIA

Nothing is ever the same
Everything is just beginning

We moved into the suburbs of Adelaide and within a few weeks my brothers and I headed off to our first day of school in Australia. It was February, forty degrees plus, we were wearing a uniform from the English winter, and it was the wrong colour.

"Thanks, Mum!" Everyone else wore grey. We were in thick black pants and white shirt, which apparently gave everyone the impression we were Mormons. "Thanks, Mum!"

It didn't take long to make friends, however, albeit with a bunch of misfits. We got into a few fights along the way, and we joined the local rugby team. Andrew, Chris, and I had played rugby union in England and now we all played in the same team for Southern Suburbs Rugby club. I loved the physicality of the game, and we were coached by an excellent sports teacher from our school. He liked to tell us that rugby union was an animal's game played by gentlemen and would constantly remind us it was not the other way around. However, a few years later, that game we loved to play was the death of my older brother Andrew.

We discovered surfing and started spending hours and hours in the sea, sometimes all day. We would catch lifts with friends or older brothers of friends, and sometimes catch buses, trains or walk long distances, any way possible, and we were in the ocean. Once you get a taste, you can't get it out your system. I already had saltwater in my veins.

The family started receiving visits from two young Mormon men who were friendly and good fun. They seemed to enjoy hanging out with the family, as they had volunteered for two years away in another country. I think they were a little homesick. One night they mentioned they knew a South Australian bodybuilding champion who was just up the road, with his own gym. They asked me if I would like to check it out and meet him. I liked the idea of being strong and I wanted to stop getting pushed around by my much bigger brother Andrew.

I went up the next night with my new Mormon friends and immediately hit it off with Karl. To a fourteen-year-old boy, Karl was very impressive to look at. He was in his early thirties and, as I found out later, a bit of a deviant. I immediately started training five nights a week for about two-and-a-half hours a night. I trained as hard and as heavy as I could, and after six months or so I could lift huge weights. There were people there who were twice my age, and I could match them or go heavier.

Karl took me under his wing and really seemed to enjoy mentoring me. We spent a lot of time together training and talking diet, health, fitness, and surfing. I met Karl's wife, Lauren, who was quite attractive, with long blonde hair and a slim body. She also worked out regularly, usually preferring the stretches that required her to bend over a lot. Lauren, as it turned out, was batshit crazy, slightly dangerous, and a nymphomaniac - not that I knew what a nymphomaniac was, but I was about to find out! Every weekday evening, I would ride my bike up a long, steep hill to their house and gym. They lived on the grounds of one of Adelaide's most prestigious private girls' schools and Karl was the head groundsman. It was going to get messy!

One evening, they planned to finish training early and go to the drive-in cinema to celebrate Karl's birthday. I was invited, but as I hopped into their van, Karl calmly walked over and said, "Hey guys, I can't go; the babysitter's cancelled. You guys go and have a good time."

"No," I said, "it's your birthday! We can stay here and do something else."

Lauren chimed in, "No, Simon, it's okay. Karl has a friend coming over. Let's go."

It was a set up. I found out later that Karl was having sex with their babysitter, a 15-year-old student at the school. She was also the young sister of my sister's boyfriend, who was training with Karl. I did say it was going to get messy, didn't I?

So yeah, you can probably guess what happened next. As we headed off to the movies in a Kombi van, I thought I had an idea of what was coming. Well, I didn't. I had not even had sex before; well, not with another person anyway. I was intrigued and nervous. I mean, I had hardly stopped thinking about sex for a couple of years, but I was a fourteen-year-old kid with a woman in her thirties, who was married to my mentor and friend. I was a little scared and tried to call the whole thing off by suggesting she drop me home on the way, that's how naive I was. As though Lauren was going to drop me off and go to the movies on her own!

As soon as we left the house, it didn't really matter what I said as Lauren was having none of it. She was absolutely in control. We arrived at the drive-in and, of course, headed straight for the back corner of the park where it was nice and dark. There were very few cars anyway, which was fortunate, because she didn't half make a racket. She had a very excitable personality, to say the least.

I can't remember what the movie was called, but it was an Aussie movie and as was usually the case, a bit B-grade with plenty of fucking in it. Back in the Kombi van the tension was palpable, the atmosphere electric. I already had an erection. My mind was racing but at least, for the time being, it was only my thoughts that were exploding. I was lying there thinking, *Oh my god, what do I do? She wants to have sex, but what to do? Maybe I should jump out of the van and run away!*

Lauren interrupted my thoughts by grabbing hold of my balls and squeezing hard. I remember thinking, *Why is she doing that? Ow! I might need them one day. Ow! Is this normal? This is weird. I wonder if they can burst like a cherry tomato.* "Simon, do you think you're old enough?"

"Er, yes, yes I, er, think so." I kept going: "Um, do you think it would be all right if you stop crushing my balls now, please?"

"Well, I think you're ready. And I am going to show you something." She rolled over and took her clothes off.

"Okay!" I squeaked.

It was over in seconds, of course; but we weren't going anywhere, and after a few more goes, I sort of started to get the hang of it. Lauren was having a lovely time and took great pleasure instructing me on what to do. She seemed to relish slapping me around the face, calling me names, screaming, laughing, and making a right meal of it. For a moment, I thought she might be possessed. Of course, I had no reference point and wondered if this was what everyone did. Was this normal?

She dropped me a few hundred yards away from home. It was very late, and she just said, "Simon, don't you tell anyone. Remember, you're mine now."

"Yes, okay." I walked off, thinking, *Yeah, I won't tell anyone, because no one would believe me anyway.*

I was a bit confused, and I felt a little guilty. I wasn't sure if I had done something wrong, not that I had much choice in the matter. I sneaked into the house, took a shower, and went to bed. I had school the next day and I had to focus on not failing Year Eight!

I surfed every chance I could, and it felt natural for me to be in the water. I won the kneeboarding state titles and headed off to the Australian schoolboy championships in Victoria, in a bus with about fifteen other kids. Our two adult guardians were two surfers in their late twenties and early thirties. I had been in Australia less than two years and still had a strong Mancunian accent. It must have made me stand out. It was a ten-hour trip, but I couldn't speak without being mimicked. Everyone joined in and had a go at the accent, but instead of it being just a bit of banter, it was designed to ridicule, and it got quite nasty. It was a real eye-opener for me as there was no team spirit, let alone camaraderie; and until then, I thought I was the only one who didn't have an accent.

On the first night we stayed in the famous surfing town of Torquay. We had our first practice surf and went to a motel. Because I was the target, I decided to stay silent almost the entire time, though ultimately that didn't help. The first I knew something was seriously wrong was when the door to my room flung open and everybody – and I mean everybody, including the adults – burst into my room and grabbed me. I jumped onto a table, and I had a second when I could have kicked one of them in the face and busted his head open. But it was a big call and I hesitated. I was hoping that perhaps whatever was going to happen would turn out to be just a bit of fun. I regret that decision now. I could have and should have used violence. I let them pull me down. They were all laughing, egging each other on, and they were enjoying themselves. The two adults bravely stepped forward, and Roger the elder of the two, said, "Hold him down, get him on the ground. Turn the pom over!"

I thought the adults were there to put an end to it, but they were the instigators. They helped by throwing me to the floor. I started to really struggle, but a few of them were kneeling on my back, some others had my arms and legs, and someone was kneeling on my head. It was getting difficult to breathe. And then one of the adults pulled my shorts down and squeezed a tube of toothpaste into my rectum. They all cheered. It was like *Lord of the Flies*. They walked out the room congratulating each other. Of course, it burnt like hell, and washing it off made it worse. I tried to make light of it and act like I didn't care, but it was humiliating, and I wanted revenge. I would have that revenge, out in the desert, a few years later, at least with some of them. I regret not confronting the two adults. I didn't mention it to anyone, not even my parents.

Most of the people on the trip were from the same surf club on the mid coast, where the swell comes into a shallow gulf. The waves there are slow, small, and inconsistent. The good surf in South Australia is hundreds of miles away in the remote bush and deserts of the Yorke Peninsula, Eyre Peninsula, and west coast. Over there it's a lifestyle. The waves are huge, powerful, beautiful, and dangerous. So are the sharks. That was where I was headed. But first, I was going to surf South Africa.

After the schoolboys' surfing trip, I went back to weight-lifting and training with even more determination. I had started lifting huge weights, especially for a fourteen-year-old. Lauren would usually find a reason to give me a lift home and give me another workout in the car, sometimes out the front of my house. I was getting nervous that my parents would find out and I was also confused about Karl knowing, but not caring. I had no idea he was having sex with their fifteen-year-old babysitter. I tried talking to Lauren, but the more I threatened to quit training, the more demanding and erratic Lauren's behaviour became.

While we were sitting out the front of my house one night, I just blurted out, "Look, Lauren, this has got to stop; we will get caught."

"No, Simon, we aren't doing anything wrong. It's natural. I like it and I need you."

"What about Karl?"

"Oh, we can have a threesome if you want."

"What! No, I didn't mean that. I meant he's going to get really mad."

"Don't be silly, he's fine. All he cares about is training and he thinks sex is draining and prevents him from bulking up."

One night, instead of turning into my street, Lauren decided she was going to take me to a popular lookout in the hills where couples go for sex. Without saying a word, she turned left instead of right and headed up the freeway in a car which was owned by the school. A few miles up the freeway, Lauren was working herself into a frenzy. She put her foot to the floor, and suddenly we were gunning up the road at eighty miles per hour. I was feeling uneasy to say the least and asked her to slow down. She ignored me. I asked her to stop and let me out. She just laughed and went faster.

I knew we were going to get wiped out, and sure enough, on the next big open bend, near the notorious crash site of Devil's Elbow, the car started to drift. We were doing some crazy speed, and with the tyres making a horrible screeching sound, the car drifted sideways. Lauren over-corrected and we shot off the road, head-on into the wall. The impact was horrendous. There were no airbags, and I wasn't wearing a seatbelt. I could see what was coming and had just enough time to cover my head before slamming into the dashboard. My door flew open, and I was thrown out of the vehicle. I was in the dirt and on my back, with my right foot caught in the seat belt.

The car had crashed into the bank, leaving the front of the car completely caved in. To make things worse, the car started to roll backward towards the road, dragging me along with it. I kicked and struggled to free my leg, but it didn't help and I was dragged across the freeway on my back. The car plunged over the edge of an embankment, taking me with it, to what I thought would be my death. Luckily, just a few metres down, the car wedged itself between some trees and stuck fast. I had managed to kick myself away from the wheels of the car, but I had generally been thrown around like a rag doll. I was bleeding, bruised and grazed but alive, with nothing broken.

Lauren climbed out of the car and helped me untangle my foot from the seat belt. She was shaken and upset but remarkably unharmed. She gave me a hug and said, "Oh, Simon, I'm so sorry! I thought I had killed you."

"I'm okay," I said, shaking like a leaf.

"Kiss me, Simon."

"What! No way! I've gotta get help! Bloody hell, you nearly killed us!"

"No, Simon, lie down. I want to fuck you. Please, Simon, fuck me now!"

"What! No, Lauren! The police will be on their way, the car's a wreck and it's probably going to burst into flames any minute! I'm going to go and get Karl." I did say she was crazy, didn't I?

She tried to push me down onto the bonnet of the car, but there wasn't even a bonnet to lie down on. it was completely mangled. She went to kiss me, but I pushed her away. I climbed up the bank onto the road and flagged down the first car I saw. I got dropped off about halfway back to their house and ran the rest of the way as fast I could. I told Karl what had happened, and he told me to go home and throw my clothes out because they were shredded and covered in blood.

"Simon, do not let your parents see you."

I just nodded and left. The next morning, I concocted an elaborate story which involved me going headfirst over the handlebars of my bike. I even smashed up my bike and bent the wheel, leaving it where my parents could see it. I didn't want to get caught. That would happen later!

It's Just the Beginning

Wheels of fate and mystery
Eternity of time
Immortality
Hold her in your hands
Throw her to the stars
Written in the sand
Washed in the dark
Hidden in a flower
Secrets from the past
Take her with you
Hold her in your arms
Looking for a heaven
Filled with the stars
It's just beginning
The end is the start
In the city you can't see
The moon of a night
Deep blue seas
What lies beneath your feet
Look away from your tv screen
So do it now
Feel what's right
Do you care about your life?
Lie down on your bed
 Just a few crumbs in your head.

Chapter Three

SOUTH AFRICA

*It doesn't matter where you come
from, just where you're going*

I flew out of Adelaide a couple of weeks after my fifteenth birthday, with a backpack and a surfboard. I was travelling with a nineteen-year-old fitness fanatic called Reno. As soon as we arrived in South Africa, I went surfing while Reno went travelling. I was there to surf the waves in and around Durban, which were well known for being world class. I stayed in a very small, dirty room at the YMCA, not five minutes' walk from the beach and surf. It was 1978, a time of apartheid in South Africa.

Durban appeared strangely familiar. Apart from the surf, it was similar to Adelaide, stuck in a time warp, a bit weird, and bloody hot. It wasn't my idea to go to South Africa, but to a fifteen-year-old kid, it sounded exciting. I was looking forward to surfing every day as I was not enjoying school and probably failing at everything anyway. Mum and Dad, who were still trying to make their marriage work, met a guy in Queensland who had plans to sail his family to South Africa on his home-made yacht. They asked him if I could join them and then told me about it! A week before we were due to leave, there was a huge cyclone in Cairns, where the boat was being fitted out and stocked with supplies. The yacht broke its moorings and sank. It was probably a good thing for everybody, including me, as I wasn't all that sure the guy had much experience or was even a competent sailor.

When that adventure failed, my parents suggested going to South Africa by plane. It was very strange, now I think about it, to send your fifteen-year-old son out to apartheid South Africa to do a spot of surfing.

The YMCA in 1978 was a hotbed of drugs, criminals, prostitutes, the mentally ill and paedophiles. It was bedlam from day one. The last thing Mum gave me as I was leaving was a diary. I still have that diary today. It's like reading an Enid Blyton novel: a bit boring, very polite, and completely fictional! There I was, the new arrival, tall, fair, extremely young and (apart from my misadventures with Lauren) very naive. As you can imagine, it did not take long to fall in with the wrong crowd, mainly because everyone there was the wrong crowd.

I had only been there a few days when two men in their mid to late twenties walked into my room and said, "Get out of bed, get dressed and meet us downstairs. Hurry up, let's go! Oh, I'm Ampie; this cunt here is Butch. We have a job for you. We gunna wait in the car. What are you waiting for? Hurry up!"

I didn't say a word. I was a bit freaked out, but I got up and went downstairs. I had seen these guys about the place. You couldn't miss them. They were two very loud and cocky Afrikaners and they had trouble written all over them. I walked out the front door and into the street.

Butch ambled over and said, "Get in the car." Seeing as I was a kid on my own in a foreign country, I did what I was told. I slid into the back seat of a large, loud sedan. Butch and Ampie started talking at the same time, explaining why I needed protection and how they were prepared to help me, if I could help them.

I hadn't been in Africa long, so I wasn't sure what I needed protection from, but I just nodded and muttered, "Okie doke." And apparently, just like that, we had an agreement. They didn't mention what it was they needed from me, and I didn't think to ask. I would find out soon enough.

We drove around for quite some time while they asked me all sorts of questions about my age, where I was from, why I was on my own, why Durban, whether I liked girls, etc. When I told them I was fifteen they burst into fits of laughter. After that day whenever they introduced me, they'd always giggle and say, "Go on, tell 'em how old you are." They were like African wild dogs.

I was sitting in the middle of the back. Butch was driving like a maniac and took every corner at high speed and sideways, as though we were being chased. I figured they were testing me out and seeing if I would freak out. They were having a great time and looking back, I realise they must have been drugged to the eyeballs. I just pretended everything was dandy and completely normal. I tried to appear relaxed as I slid from one side of the car to the other, while we drove through red lights at a hundred mph in the city centre on a Saturday morning. We saw no police and they had absolutely no regard for anyone else on the road.

They dropped me back at the YMCA. "We'll see you later, English."

"Yeah, no worries." I was worried, I just didn't want to show it, I think I instinctively knew that to look scared or show any sort of weakness would have made things worse. I knew they were no good, but I didn't know how to get rid of them.

That night, they found me in the dining area witnessing one of the residents have an extremely bad seizure. I had talked to this young man a few times, usually late at night. He wouldn't take his medication; he was a loner and would sit up all night in the foyer. He died a few weeks later in the TV room, while I watched in horror. Ampie and Butch walked in as if they owned the place.

"Get in the car, English. We're going to a club. Don't worry 'bout the retard. Let's go."

We walked out and as expected, took off at breakneck speed. Butch owned the road until we pulled into a grimy, dark back alley. Butch parked in the middle of the alley (apparently he owned that too) and we headed up some stairs with boxes of records, and a pretty girl let us into the back door of a nightclub. It seemed Ampie was a DJ and he was going to be spinning records. As the night went on and people packed in, I was given the job of distributing small packets of white powder to certain people in exchange for cash, which seemed to make me very popular. Everyone was having a good time. It was a real party. The girls looked beautiful, and everyone was dancing. I didn't ask what the drug was, but it was being snorted, so I presume it was cocaine.

Ampie had given me instructions. "Right, English, there's the baggies, they're twenty rand each and you sell as many as you can, stay close, and keep buying me drinks. You hold onto the money until the end of the night. Easy, right, English?"

"Okay, Ampie. You sure this is okay?"

He laughed, "Don't worry 'bout it, English. This is our club and this is Durban, *ja*?"

I was the only sober one there. It was very early morning when we packed up. I was exhausted and I needed to sleep, but I knew the surf would be good early and I wasn't going to miss a great swell, offshore winds, and a good tide. I surfed most days. For a fifteen-year-old kid in Durban in the '70s, there wasn't much else to do. There was one television with one channel at the YMCA, mostly in Afrikaans, and it was only on for a few hours a day. Butch and Ampie showed up when they wanted me to either do the clubs, drop packages off, and/or run errands during the day. It was all organised from one of the rooms in the YMCA, and it was always busy.

I asked for their help once and immediately regretted it. I was getting harassed by two older men staying at the YMCA, which was extra weird because I thought the YMCA was for young men and they were in their 40s and 50s. One day they got a bit aggressive and propositioned me for sex several times in the usually quiet television room. I left but freaked out when they followed me into the lift. They stood in front of the lift doors, to prevent me from getting out, but luckily a few of Butch's crew came out of a room and got into the lift. They realised what was happening and let me out. I went to see Ampie and Butch straightaway and asked them to help. They got up immediately,

"Let's go, English. We'll pay them a visit."

We went straight to their room and instead of knocking or opening the door, Ampie just kicked it and tore it open. The two men were sitting on the end of their beds, and they jumped up in shock and started to say, "We don't want any trouble."

Butch, who usually did most of the talking, became extremely aggressive and started shouting.

"Shut the fuck up, queer!"

He grabbed one of the men and pulled out a knife. Ampie joined in with relish and started yelling something in Afrikaans. He jumped onto a chair and kicked the older man in the face, sending blood spraying up the wall. I froze. Butch and Ampie were enjoying themselves. It got ugly very quickly. I told them I was leaving and headed for the doorway.

Ampie yelled at me, "Hey English, get back here! This is for you."

"Let's go. That's enough. They won't bother me again. Let's go." I ran out of the room, out the front door and down to the ocean.

One of the men went to hospital in an ambulance. I could see the main road from my bedroom window, and late that night I saw the other man load up a car and leave. I felt terrible but I had no-one to talk to. There were no police called. I rarely saw any police and I started to wonder if they might be as bad as Butch and Ampie. After that incident, if I wasn't surfing, I stayed in my room, even avoiding mealtimes. The YMCA in Durban in the '70s was a dangerous place to be.

The nineteen-year-old with whom I had flown out of Australia returned from his Cape Town trip and shared a room with me. We bought a very old car for sixty rand. It ran rough and leaked oil like a sieve, but it got us into Swaziland. We drove into the mountains, toured a few wildlife parks, and on our way back to Durban, stopped to give a local black man a ride home. Apparently, you were not really allowed to do such things.

I got out of the car and let him in. "Hi there. Do you want a lift?" He looked a bit surprised to say the least, but just grinned at me. And I said, "Hop in, let's go."

He climbed into the back and started laughing. He smiled, grinned, and laughed just about all the way. There we were, two scruffy kids from another world, driving a beat-up, smoky bomb on a dirt road in the middle of nowhere. It was getting late in the day when we pulled up outside a small township, surrounded by a fence and barbed wire.

Our new friend got out and said, "Please wait. Wait here, please. I will come back." He jumped through a hole in the fence and ran off. A few minutes later he came running back with a beaming smile, some home brew and about fifty other people, all of whom seemed to think it was all very funny and exciting, which it was. Of course, when it was time to leave, the car wouldn't start, which had everyone in hysterics. They pushed us up the road and off we went in a cloud of dust, filthy exhaust smoke and a whole lot of fanfare. I will never forget that man's face. He lived in a hovel within a camp surrounded by barbed wire, worked underground in a mine, was dirt poor and probably owned nothing, yet he had some life about him that I hadn't recognised in many people.

Back in Durban I got into a routine of surfing and trying to avoid Ampie and Butch, but nothing really worked as they would just come to my room late at night, make me get out of bed, and off we would go. I wasn't so sure why they needed me. I think partly they thought it was amusing to have a kid around selling their drugs for them, and maybe it was good for business. I don't know. Whatever the reason was, we were very busy, and the drug trade was lucrative. We would pull up somewhere, they would wait in the car while I delivered whatever it was, I would get the cash, give it to Ampie, and off we'd go to the next drop, usually with Butch driving like a demon harbouring a death wish. On one of the runs, we spotted some guys from a rival gang hanging about in an underground car park. Butch pulled up next to them, and Ampie pulled out a large fire extinguisher he'd stolen and drowned them in a sea of white dust and foam. As it emptied, he threw the bottle at them, and we took off whooping and hollering. It was like the wild west.

The YMCA was pretty much in the middle of the city. I would walk through the streets to do some food shopping once or twice a week, usually in bare feet, t-shirt and boardies. I think one gentleman in an expensive-looking suit and tie must have thought I was homeless because he very kindly offered me fifteen rand to have sex with him. To tell you the truth, it was such a small amount, I was slightly insulted. I must have been adapting to the environment because that was the first thought that popped into my head. *What? Only fifteen rand? My bottom's worth more than that, surely!*

I politely refused, and as I turned around to walk away, he grabbed me by the hair and, pulling me backwards, growled, "How dare you turn your back on me? Don't you walk away." I looked into his eyes and felt a chill. They were glazed and dark. He looked like a devil, and as if he wanted to kill me. He grabbed my arm and backhanded me across the face. He was a big, tall man, heavy set, in his early forties, and he had a strong hold on me while he dragged me towards his car. I suddenly felt a surge of rage explode in me. I seemed to morph into a wild animal fighting for its life which, by the look on the man's face, took him completely by surprise. I went batshit crazy and screamed at him, tore myself free, and ran into the middle of the road. I stopped the traffic and sprayed a torrent of abuse at him. It felt like the whole city was watching. He looked horrified, jumped in his car and took off! He should have tried chocolates and flowers, or dinner even. No wonder they say romance is dead.

Some of the surf in South Africa really is world class, and I spent a lot of time in the water. While my friends were going through high school, I was surfing. Well, that is what I wrote home. I didn't mention to anyone what was really going on. The food at the YMCA was terrible, practically unfit for human consumption. It was only a matter of time before I fell seriously ill with chronic food poisoning. I'm not sure why, but I didn't go to a doctor, hospital or even a chemist, which now seems crazy. I was deteriorating badly and after three weeks of chronic vomiting and diarrhoea, I decided to leave. I caught a plane to England and went straight to my grandparents, who took me to hospital, where of course I was diagnosed with a severe case of gastroenteritis.

I arrived back in the UK in late summer and, after I recovered, found work on a farm just outside Macclesfield. I discovered a taste for alcohol and went out with friends most evenings, or to be exact, went out and got absolutely smashed. I would drive home in the very early morning on a stolen, but very fast, go-kart. It was brilliant fun. It even had room for a passenger if they stood on the back and hung onto me! I also borrowed a nice sports car with a friend one night. We just walked up a very posh driveway on a very posh street and found the keys in the ignition. We picked up two lovely-looking, fun girls and headed off for a drive in the country. I was a considerate car thief, however, and returned the vehicle in reasonable condition, with a complimentary pair of knickers on the back seat, albeit a little low on fuel.

The people I was staying with had noticed I was up to mischief and decided they had seen enough of me. They were justifiably a bit concerned about their twin daughters, who were my age and just as curious as I was. They took me to a house in Manchester where one of Dad's friends lived with a housemate; they were both professional guys in their early thirties.

Anyway, there was not much to do in that area, especially for a fifteen-year-old with no school, no work, and no friends. I was not impressed; in fact, it was annoying. One minute I was living in a small but impressive mansion with the twins, and with a souped-up go-kart in the garage, and the next minute I was in a horrible little house in a grim suburb of Manchester. The house was empty during the day as both the guys worked on their careers, so I cranked up the stereo, or at least I did until I discovered the housemate had a world class collection of vintage Playboy magazines stashed in his room.

I was very careful. I mean, the collection looked valuable, it was stored carefully and kept in excellent condition. One day when I was very bored, I decided to get them all out, remove the centerfolds and carefully lay the pictures on the floor. It took about an hour until I was standing in the middle of a hundred centrefolds. They were beautiful. Okay, look, I know. But hey, I was fifteen and beggars can't be choosers. The tension was palpable. I couldn't wait any longer; I took it out and in one big perverse explosion ejaculated all over the pictures. A few moments passed and I regained my composure. As I stood there with dick in hand, the realisation of what I had done began to dawn on me. *Oh my god, I'm dead. He's going to kill me - what am I going to do?*

I ran downstairs and rang some family friends. I concocted a story about being scared and lonely and begged them to come and pick me up. It seemed to work because they said they would be round in a couple of hours. I ran back upstairs and chucked everything I owned in my backpack and then went back to the room where the devil had possessed me! I was in a bit of a panic, so I rather carelessly put all the photos randomly back into the magazines. Well, it wasn't as if he'd be flicking through those pages ever again. I put them back in his room, grabbed my pack and waited outside, at the other end of the street, never to return. Oh, the shame!

A few months later, word got back home that I was up to no good and I received a phone call from Father instructing me to get back to Adelaide immediately!

Could I but live again

I would turn from ambition and teach no-one

Creating life in a quiet place

Meant for giving

Moments of grace

Stand alone

Watch birds fly

Never a need in thine eyes

Wanters abound, mocked by sun

Free to forgo, never undone

Discernment I see

In shadow of fire

Cast aside, bound in desire

Waking to hope

Trust in my dream

Gentle waters that I've never seen

Lies within power

The jewel in one

Earth, stars, moon and sun

Here I stay

With closed eyes

Touching faith

Live or die

Chapter Four

THE STORM CREATES THE RIDE

Let the heathens Rage
And the People
Imagine Vain things
In times betrayal
Cleave with fires peril
To the beating of your Heart

Back in Adelaide, I was still too young to drive legally, and with all my friends in school, I decided to find a job, just until I could get a driver's licence and take off. I got a crappy job at a large bicycle, camping and gun store called Super Elliott's in the city.

My dad came into the store one afternoon completely out the blue and asked me to leave work and go with him and my brothers to the airport. I hopped in the back behind Dad, and he drove us to the airport in silence. I wondered what was going on and looked at Chris for a hint. I could tell from the look on everyone's faces it wasn't going to be good. I kept quiet and said nothing. We pulled up at the airport. Dad hopped out of the car and grabbed his briefcase, and Andrew jumped into the driver's seat.

The windows were down and – I will never forget this moment for the rest of my life – Dad just leant down, and said, "Me and your mother are getting a divorce." He looked a little choked up. That was it. He turned around and walked away. No explanation, no discussion and no "Sorry boys, I still love you and things will be okay!"

Chris and Andrew burst into tears, and I should have joined them, let it all out, let it go, but I didn't. I was a bit shocked and angry. I think I was staying silent in childish protest, as a kind of "No, I'm not going to let you hurt me. Not that badly, anyway". Silly and irrational, I know. I wish I had cried it out, but I bottled it up. It would eat away at me later. I sat in the back of the car and stayed quiet. No-one said a word. Andrew slowly got it together and drove home, everyone went to their rooms and shamefully, we all walked past Mum, who was sitting at the dinner table by herself, white as a ghost. I deeply regret not sitting down with her that day. I could have given her a hug and I should have told her how much I loved her.

Dad moved to Sydney and my sister followed. My brothers and I were sent to stay with different families in Adelaide. Mum disappeared and I am pretty sure she had a mental breakdown. I went to live with my friend Kyle and his family, who had emigrated from Scotland, and I lost touch with all my family for quite some time.

I didn't hear from Dad either, but of course Lauren tracked me down. She would wait out the front of the house for everyone to leave and let herself in to have sex with me while her young children waited in the car. It was very weird, and the father of my friend was a little scary. He was an officer in the army and an old school military man. I hate to think what would have happened if he had caught me with Lauren in the house.

I was almost 16 and I wanted to run away, I just had to wait a little longer for my freedom ticket, aka driver's licence. It was at about this time that Kyle introduced me to marijuana. According to Kyle, smoking a shitload of cannabis was not bad for you in any shape or form, and I was informed on several occasions that quite incredibly, it was good for you! It'd go something like this: "Come on, Hartley. You gotta try it. It's really good stuff, mate. They've done experiments. Come on, this shit, it's actually good for you, it's not like the ciggies."

It was escapism and I enjoyed it, pretty much like everyone else around me. I started to smoke every day. It was cheap, easy to buy, and it was everywhere. South Australia's climate is perfect for growing marijuana, and back then SA supplied most of the other states in Australia. SA also had very liberal and relaxed laws regarding cannabis, thanks to a Premier from the '70s called Don Dunstan. Whether that was a good thing or not, I don't know! Even our police were a bit more laid back, especially compared to NSW and Queensland, where there was a lot more corruption and organised crime.

Adelaide was just a big country town, with a population of about one million.

I spent the next few months dodging Lauren (that's dodging Lauren, not dogging Lauren), chasing girls my own age, surfing, and getting stoned. I got my licence the moment I turned 16, and with no hesitation headed out west to the desert, wilderness, surf, and freedom. I moved out there with a mate called Zac who had been born and raised in Papua New Guinea. He had moved to Adelaide around the same time as me and he was a natural surfer.

The first winter we got lucky and found a shack on the beach with the bare essentials - two beds, a long drop and a teapot. We surfed every day we could. If there was no swell, we would fish or dive for fish; and I hiked into the bush and planted cannabis. There was very little water and no rain in summer, so I had to stick close to the dirt roads and tracks. I would carry bore water in large plastic containers using a backpack and holding a container in each hand. The crops were well hidden in remote areas, and I would have a long walk to carry the water they needed, sometimes up to half a mile or so through thick bush.

My main concern was not to be seen by anyone, especially the local Park Ranger, who seemed to think he was Rambo! He knew what I was doing and desperately wanted to catch me red-handed. A couple of times a year he would organise a helicopter and fly over the bush, close to the roads and tracks. He had some tracking skills too, so I had to be super careful not to leave footprints in the sand. I'd cover my tracks by walking backwards on my way out and using brush to wipe away any footprints.

I wasn't the only one growing in that area and the Ranger would occasionally have some success, find some crops, and make a bust. This encouraged him to keep looking and bring in more resources, including police and detectives from Adelaide. After one summer, the Ranger had found so many crops that his shed was full of plants. However, instead of burning them, he sold them to a guy I knew quite well, and the marijuana was taken to Adelaide and sold for a small fortune. I couldn't believe it. Mr High-and-Mighty had been moaning to everyone about me growing dope in the park, and now he had gone over to the dark side!

The police would come over all the way from Adelaide. They never had much luck busting me, mainly because the crops were way out in the bush and they were never going to catch me onsite, especially as I did the watering at night. The big risk for me was after harvesting, when I had to take it by car hundreds of miles to Adelaide.

The quality of the crop was always exceptional as I had great seeds, and apart from the lack of water, the bush was a perfect environment for growing cannabis. The plants had direct sun all day, protection from strong winds, and sandy, well-drained soil. I never had any problems moving the dope, and for good money. I had just two big buyers. One was a bike gang and the other was a guy who had contacts all over

Australia with organised crime. He also owned an infamous hotel on the main strip in Adelaide called The Century, but I will get to that later. I could never prove it, but I am convinced he worked for the Federal Police.

On one of my runs to Adelaide, I had arranged a big sale in advance, but the crop had not dried in time. I decided to throw the plants, roots and all, into large cardboard boxes and packed them into the back of my beat-up station wagon. At the last minute, Zac asked me to give his girlfriend, Cindy, a lift to Adelaide. I didn't think anything of it; I just cranked up the stereo and headed off.

I was in another world and too stoned to think or even care about the consequences. The cops were aware of what I was doing. They just didn't have the details, and I always seemed to slip through the net. I saw Cindy a few months later and to my surprise she explained how nerve-wracking it had been for her. Apparently, driving hundreds of miles in a car full of six-foot cannabis plants can give you a touch of anxiety. I hadn't given it a thought. As far as I was concerned, it was all quite normal.

I was fairly cashed up by now. I was single and I didn't need a lot of stuff. All I needed were a few essentials to travel up and down the coast, chasing the best waves. So long as I had food, water, surfboard and wetsuit, I was happy. I had a bit of basic fishing stuff and some good diving gear for spearfishing. I dived a lot, but unlike some, I would only shoot what I could eat at the next meal. There was plenty of great fish to choose from, including crayfish,flathead, groper and abalone.

In winter I would sleep in a tent or in my car; and in summer I would sleep anywhere, next to the fire or in the sand dunes. For quite a few years, I didn't own a tent, swag, sleeping bag or pillow. I slept in my surfboard cover and used whatever was on hand to make a reasonably comfortable bed. I didn't have to worry about anyone or anything. Having said that, I was increasingly thinking about the opposite sex (sometimes known as girls), and that would mean spending time in the city.

It was around this time that I bought an acoustic guitar. I had always loved music. My car stereo was worth more than my car, and as I got older music became more and more important to me. I had plenty of time when the winds blew onshore, and soon I was obsessed with surfing, music and playing guitar. I started taking more and more trips to Adelaide, usually to jam with friends and chase girls.

One night I went to visit a friend who, like most kids our age, still lived at home with his mum and his very weird older brother. That's not me being a bit judgmental; no, he grew up to become a murderer. Anyway, stop interrupting, it's getting annoying. While I was there, I was introduced to a slightly scary woman in her early thirties. She looked a bit goth, or maybe it was Halloween – I can't remember. Anyway, the point is, she was renting a cottage out the back. She asked me to give her a hand moving some furniture and two minutes later she said, "Simon, can I seduce you?"

About five seconds later, we were having sex! What was I going to say? "Oh dear, we've only just met, don't you think we should get to know each other first?" Or maybe, "Are you a witch?" I was going to ask her if she wanted me to dress up as a vampire or whatnot, but she jumped me before I got a chance.

The next day I hit the road, but a couple of days later, I was in agony, urinating razor blades. The doctor's words rang in my head as I walked out of his office. "You should choose your partners more carefully, young man. That's a nasty STD you have there. Now go and give her the good news and take your damn pills."

A week later, I was standing on another stunning beach, hundreds of miles away. I was hanging around with some friends, a mixed bunch of surfers, fishermen, dropouts, and lost souls. We thought we had nothing to do. The surf was flat. I can't remember whose idea it was, but someone suggested we steal a boat and go for a spin in the bay (as you do). It was a particularly good day for stealing boats. We had clear waters, no wind, and the bay was nicely protected from the open ocean. The cray fishing season had just finished too, so there was no-one around.

Like I said, perfect conditions for stealing a boat. We broke into a shed, got a motor sorted and pushed a large tinny into the bay. Three of us hopped in and Gopher (yes, we called him that because he looked like a Gopher) took the helm and we sped off at full throttle. About half a mile out to sea we hit a bit of swell, and as we were all sitting on the edge of the boat, it almost flipped, coming right up on a steep angle. It instantly threw the guy opposite me into the water, and with his weight gone my side of the boat came down hard and flipped me into the water. Gopher was thrown out at the same time, narrowly missing the outboard engine and propeller.

I came up and thought, "That's strange." The boat had kept going. The engine was jammed at full throttle, and it was going to keep running until it ran out of fuel and yes, you guessed it, Gopher had just filled the tank. We were quite a long way out to sea, with no wetsuits or life jackets, and as we surfaced, we saw the boat was going very fast with no-one in it. At first the boat appeared to be racing off towards the horizon but as we watched, it hit some chop and changed direction. Before we knew what was happening, it turned around at full speed and headed straight for us.

I feared someone was going to get mangled. It was a good thing we didn't have life jackets on, because the only way to avoid the boat and its propeller was to dive for the bottom. It was hard to see without goggles, but you could hear the engine of the boat zoom overhead. I would hold my breath for as long as I could, then shoot up to the surface. It was bizarre; the boat looked like it was being controlled remotely from the shore by some psycho who wanted us dead.

It just kept coming at us, through us and over us again and again. It felt like we were being hunted, and the boat's movement was completely unpredictable. Each time I surfaced it would be with the utmost trepidation, hoping the boat, that had just passed overhead, would not swing around and immediately head straight back. When I dived down, I feared the propeller would catch my feet, and every time I came up, I feared my head would get lopped off. I was treading water and keeping an eye on it as much as possible, but after a few minutes it was starting to get very tiring, and what started out as a bit of a laugh was turning into a nightmare. I was staying down less and less, to save energy, but the boat kept circling. Finally, it hit a home run and we watched it head out to sea. Exhausted, we started a long and slow swim back to the beach. At least there were no sharks around.

Meanwhile, I was still getting letters from Lauren, but because I hadn't replied, she had the brilliant idea of sending a letter to my mum's address. Mum opened the letter straight away, as she had already become a bit suspicious of Lauren over the years; and sure enough, it was a rather nasty letter, with explicit and sordid details of some of our past encounters. It was also threatening and demanding. She insisted I stop ignoring her.

Mum left a message at the trading post fifty miles away and asked me to call her. There was only one phone, and it was so old that it had a handle which you had to wind up. The operator, who lived in the little house next to the phone box, would then put you through and listen in! Mum was none too happy. She had already been to see Lauren and threatened to call the police and the school, where Lauren and Karl still lived.

I didn't hear from Lauren again. Well, not for a few years. Mum was so upset she put my older brother on the line. He was going to let me know just how disappointed the whole family was and, Mum hoped, give me a lecture on the morals of good behaviour. Andrew waited for Mum to leave the room and said, "You lucky bastard," then hung up.

The next day, when I went in to pay for fuel, the operator, who also ran the store, gave me a filthy look. And as she handed over my change, she couldn't help herself and mumbled, "You should be ashamed of yourself."

Life is like a river

From the ground into a stream

Twists and turns

Flows and grows

Falls into the sea

Born within the mountain

The river runs wide and deep

At first it's fast and moves in time

Reflections you can see

With age it slows and fades to dark

Constrained by gravity

Then change will come

With constant grace

A place I want to be.

Love grows bold and waterfalls

Sure as the sun does rise

Come with me and set us free

Against the pull of time

Walk through fire and

Let it rain

The wind will blow

It's all the same

Chapter Five

JOIN THE ALIENS OR JOIN THE ARMY

The light in the darkness is truth

If I had to pick just one incident that is burnt into my memory, it would be this! I was heading back to a camp site we had named Two Fish (no prizes for guessing why). I was alone, it was after midnight, and it was a pitch-black night with no moon. This was still very early '80s, so there were no mobile phones or technology. I had been driving for hours and there were rarely other vehicles on the road, especially in the early hours. This night I hadn't seen another vehicle for at least an hour. I was getting close to a place we called Ten Mile Hill (need I explain?). The road was narrow and straight with very thick scrub and bush on both sides. There was an old, rotting fence on one side of the road and the occasional wooden pole holding up a single phone line.

I was fighting off fatigue and considering whether to pull over and sleep, when in the distance I caught sight of a very bright light. It was far ahead and at first appeared quite small.

I kept driving but started slowing down. I removed my home-made cruise control, which was an octopus strap wrapped around the accelerator pedal, onto a hook and clipped onto the door handle. I won't be taking a patent out on that idea; it got stuck once going into a hairpin corner and I ended up flying through a fence and into a paddock, surprisingly in one piece, although the car looked a little worse for wear. Anyway, I pulled over. Well, I say pulled over, but I just stopped in the middle of the road. I turned off the lights and engine. It was very dark, with no wind at all, and deathly quiet. I had pulled over briefly a couple of hours earlier and marvelled at just how clear and beautiful the night sky was, jam-packed with stars and the Milky Way.

Before going further with what happened that night, I want you to know that I considered leaving this event out. I have rarely mentioned it to anyone, and when I did, I'd get the typical response one might expect. Even my closest friend at the time, fellow surfer, renegade, and desert rat, scoffed! I can understand why, of course. I never mentioned it again until now. I'll stick to the facts and relay exactly what happened or didn't happen, and you make of it what you will.

These aliens jumped out of the bushes and anal probed me! Just kidding. Settle down.

So there I was, on a deserted road in the middle of nowhere, and on my left, not fifty feet away, sitting just above the bush, perhaps thirty feet in the air, was an incredibly bright white light. The light source, whatever it was, seemed to be about twenty to thirty feet square at least, but it was hard to tell as it seemed to have no shape and it was not lighting up the area near it or around it. It was eerily silent. I got out of the car and walked over for a closer look. I was trying to look for or think of a logical explanation. My first thought was maybe it was a farmer with giant spotlights on a ridiculously huge vehicle, perhaps on a hunting trip.

"NO. Don't be stupid." I had started talking to myself. "There's no farmland here, the bush is too thick, there are too many rocks and there's no noise and no movement. Maybe it's a road crew repairing the phone line! No, there's nothing here except a light. Why is that?" There were no vehicles, nothing, just a light. It looked like a tear in the night sky. I kept on talking to myself for a minute or two, but how do you explain something you can't explain? How do you explain a hole in the night?

"What the fuck is it? What the fuck is it? What the fuck!" As you can see, it wasn't the most intelligent conservation I've ever had, and I wasn't getting any answers. I did the smartest thing I could think of and picked up a rock. I thought about throwing it. I was close enough, but I started to get a horrible feeling that it was something sinister.

So, I ask you, what has a pure white light, but doesn't light up the ground it appears to be pointing at, does not move, has no sound, seems to have nothing visibly attached to it, is as big as a small house, magically floats thirty feet off the ground, and looks as though it emanates from a tear in the night sky? I stood and stared at it for a few minutes. It was so close. I was fascinated, and I wanted to know what it was. As I moved closer, I experienced a chilling feeling that something was coming up behind me. I spun round and ran for the car. I broke into a cold sweat. I started the car and floored it. I started talking to myself again.

"The car's going to cut out, something's in the car with me, something's going to jump into the road and stop the car. What the fuck was that?"

I was totally paranoid. I really thought something, somehow, was going to stop me from leaving. I got off the main road and, driving like a maniac, I hit the dirt tracks all the way to camp, and fuck any kangaroos that might get in the way. When I got to camp there was only Thommo there, an old hippie surfer. I woke him up and told him what had happened, and he looked genuinely freaked out. I tried to get him to come back with me to investigate. I had seen something that made no sense and I really needed someone else to witness it. I wanted an explanation, but of course he said, "No way." And I wasn't going back there on my own. I think he made the right call.

I went back the next day to see if there was anything I could find, anything at all. I was good with tracking and recognising landmarks from locating crops in the bush, and I found the exact spot where I had stopped. I searched the place and found nothing. There was no sign of any human activity or vehicle access; it was just rocks and thick scrub, impossible terrain for any sort of vehicles. I couldn't even find so much as a broken twig, let alone tyre tracks.

I can remember every detail about that night as though it was yesterday. I have no explanation and never will. I do wonder if some of my more haunting and hellish nightmares are connected to that night. I still have a recurring dream about an owl and an emptiness, that I cannot put into words.

I was only a teenager, but I knew I wanted a companion, otherwise known as a girlfriend. I was on the road a heck of a lot, and spending months in places that were seriously remote. I kept returning to the city lights, which were often ten or so hours away. I tried living on the east coast one summer with a couple of friends, as the coastline there is heavily populated, and the towns and cities have plenty of surf and girls. It didn't feel right, though. I was used to the wild west coast, with empty beaches, and a completely different lifestyle that was anything but urban. The east coast girls were great, though; I think the Beach Boys wrote a song about it. I drove back to Adelaide on my own, surfing my way down the coast from Queensland, and into NSW and Victoria.

I had three real heroes as a teenager. First and foremost, the brilliant and innovative electric guitarist Jimi Hendrix; secondly, the Californian kneeboarder, board maker and surf photographer, George Greenough; and lastly, the Australian kneeboard champion and surf photographer, Peter Crawford. Peter was from Dee Why near Sydney, and if not famous, was very well known and highly respected. As a fourteen-year-old

I had seen him on television carving up some waves, amazingly for a soft drink commercial.

On my way down the coast, I stopped in Sydney and found Dee Why pumping under a huge swell. I could see Peter was out there getting tubed in front of the rocks and I excitedly paddled out. The waves that day were as big as Dee Why could handle and it was not for the inexperienced or faint-hearted. The swell was new and chaotic and on the high tide, breaking very close to the headland; one wipeout in the wrong place and you would end up on rocks, being hammered by eight-foot waves.

I noticed Peter riding higher up the wave than usual when speeding through the tube, as it was sucking the bowl dry on some of the bigger waves and exposing jagged rocks. I paddled inside everyone and took the biggest wave in a monster set. I critically left it until the last second to take off, paddling up the face of the wave, spinning round at the last split second and free-falling into the wave. The rail dug in and I flew across a huge green wall of fast-moving water. I could see the bowl section coming up almost immediately, so I manoeuvred into position to get tubed and avoid the rocks, when I saw Peter drop in and head straight for me. I remember thinking, "Wow, that's cool! Bit dangerous, but hopefully there's room for two."

The next thing I knew Peter came down the face of the wave, surfed right up to me and abruptly gave me an almighty push, knocking me off my board and onto the exposed rocks in the notorious Dee Why bowl. I got thrown around like a rag doll. I won't say I bounced off the rocks - there wasn't much bouncing. It was more like me going through a cheese grater with a few tons of water on my back. I surfaced with cuts and bruises everywhere, my wetsuit torn, surfboard damaged, and about thirty or so sea urchin spines embedded in both feet. I spent the next few hours on a hospital bed having them dug out. That experience was a tad disappointing.

When I arrived back in Adelaide, I was asked to surf for Australia at the world championships in California. I needed a new surfboard, so I said I would go if someone sponsored me. I got the sponsorship and a new board from Lipstix surfboards and headed off to California. I met the rest of the Australian team in Sydney, as I was the only one from South Australia, and we all got on well.

The trouble started when we arrived in the US. I was the only one with a British passport – it was the Australian surfing team, after all. This meant that I needed a visa. I didn't have a visa or Australian citizenship. I hadn't thought about it and no-one had asked. I ended up spending hours in a room with customs officers and eventually a diplomat. After a lot of wrangling, they let me in and I joined everyone on the bus, only to discover that my surfboard and luggage had disappeared permanently. I had no carry-on luggage, so I had nothing!

We stayed in San Diego, the surf was bloody terrible, and to top it all off, South Africa unexpectedly showed up and we were told not to compete. Politics! It was the early eighties and there was a sporting boycott of South Africa because of apartheid. I had borrowed a surfboard but wasn't enjoying the crappy surf anyway, so I really didn't care.

Things improved vastly when the team hired a bus with a few locals, including Tom Curren, and we headed down to Mexico. We hit the Baja Peninsula, which was spectacular and not unlike the west coast of South Australia. Mexico was exactly as I had imagined it. They had tacos, tequila and everything! We had some great surf with endless beaches and big swells. On the way back, I still didn't have a visa, so I got off the bus before the border and hopped in a car full of Californians, hoping we would get waved through, which we did. Well, something had to go right, didn't it?

I never competed again after that trip. Surfing for me was too much of a soulful and individual thing. Just you and the endless power of the ocean, to be immersed in the water, surrounded by nature and the rolling weather systems, all conspiring thousands of miles away to occasionally bring you perfect waves that come to an end, breaking on remote reefs and deserted beaches. It was a lifestyle, and something uniquely powerful and dangerous, an almost spiritual experience, a searching, and a kind of meditation.

It was around this time that my older brother Andrew broke his neck playing rugby for Southern Suburbs Rugby Club. By the time I got back to the city to see him, he was a ventilated quadriplegic and not expected to live more than a few weeks. In an instant, Andrew had become Australia's worst case of quadriplegia. When Andrew first arrived in emergency, the hospital made mistakes, which led to the break going from C5 to C3.

One of the hardest things I have ever done was to walk into the ICU and look him in the eyes. I didn't want to cry but I didn't know what to do, or more importantly what to say. It was harrowing and I felt overcome with sadness and even guilt. It should have been me! I was taking all the stupid risks. Andrew was the ideal son and Dad's favourite. He was the first-born male and already benefiting from a successful career in business. He was charming, tall, handsome, intelligent, and funny, and he was just twenty years old. I walked over the threshold into the ICU and up to his bed, I couldn't get one word out. What could I say? It was useless. Life seemed so unfair and shitty. I just stood there mute, with tears streaming down my face, trying to fathom the cruel brutality of life.

A few months later, without saying a word to anyone, I drove to Sydney and enlisted in the Army. Wait! What the fuck? Did what? Jesus, what the hell was I thinking?

I was nineteen and on another bus. This time, however, instead of heading off on a mystery tour of the Mexican coast, I was heading inland to Wagga Wagga, the Australian Army's headquarters for basic training. I should have followed my friends to surf the waves of Indonesia.

The first thing the Army do when you arrive is cut off all your hair and shave your head. There's a lot of shouting too.

I could see guys on the firing range let rip with automatic weapons, while the Sergeant screamed, "Kill the gook!" What did I expect? I enjoyed the physical challenges, the hiking, climbing and runs through the mountains and rivers. I wasn't the fastest man there, but I had built up incredible stamina from years of weight training and surfing. I was first back to camp every time, out of forty-two men.

However, after a few weeks, I decided that I had nothing against people of Asian descent, and I missed my guitar, music, surfing and freedom. I had made the wrong decision and I asked my commander to release me from my contract. That went down like a ton of bricks! Suddenly I was confronted by Mr Shouty Man. I was immediately separated from my squad and confined to a small room they called a holding cell. A prison cell with a nice name. They let me out during the day to do manual labour and locked me up every afternoon. I met a couple of real psychos that were banged up in the cells next to me, but I could be psycho too, so they let me be. After a few hellish weeks, I ended up back in Adelaide with my tail between my legs. I was going to stay with my mum until I worked out what to do next. She opened the door and burst into tears.

"Simon, how could you? You should have stayed. What are you going to do now? I'm so disappointed in you."

Yeah, well, I'm disappointed in me, too! I decided to find somewhere else to stay. I shacked up with a girlfriend, recruited a couple of friends, and within a few months I started a pub rock band called Blue Experience. My old school friend, Kyle, was on drums and vocals, and Eddie, an old surfing friend, was on bass and vocals, and I played guitar. We got to work. I wrote a few songs and Kyle helped with the lyrics. I became dedicated to music very quickly and practised all day every day. I played along with records, bought a few music books, and burnt the midnight oil. I over did it and my fingers swelled up.

Time for another surf trip. After a few months, I headed back to the city hoping to carve out a career in music. Ha ha. Eddie rented a cottage on a farm, and we jammed and rehearsed often. We were getting serious. Well, we were getting stoned.

I also bought a motorbike, not just any old bike, but the fastest motocross bike in the world. Someone who obviously didn't care much for their safety had modified the bike just enough to get it registered, which meant I could ride it on the road. It was a beast and it was dangerous. I could barely keep the front wheel on the ground, and of course I dropped it, crashed it, and smashed it on many occasions. However, as you may have guessed by now, unlike several of my friends, I did not kill myself.

One For the Angels

You walked down another road
It's growing dark, time to go
I hear your voice in my head
I can feel it now, your gentle breath
In your eyes you showed me why
All this time, I realised

I'll look for you in a dark night's sky
The very star that's shining bright
How your courage set you free
My love, find some peace
See you soon, brother, meet again
Don't know how, don't know when
Going back from where you came
Angels carry you home again.
Carry you home
Angels

Chapter Six

ONE FOR THE ANGELS

Like a pond
Some people just see their reflection on the surface
Others might dive in and find another world

Andrew was still in hospital in the ICU. It had been months and most of the family visited him every day. He turned twenty-one, to the surprise of the doctors. Andrew's old girl-friend Ann had also visited him every day. Ann was a nurse and decided she wanted to marry Andrew, despite his terrible injuries. They married in hospital and Dad found a house for them to turn into a home.

They were going to need some professional help on a regular basis. Andrew had survived a catastrophic injury; he couldn't move anything but his head, he couldn't breathe without a ventilator, couldn't talk, and needed a pacemaker. It still hurts to even think about how much he suffered. God knows what my mum and dad went through, and how they found the courage to carry on.

After about a week in the ICU, Andrew's heart stopped beating and the doctors gave Mum and Dad a couple of minutes to decide on whether to resuscitate him or not. Mum was against it and chose to let him go. Dad said, "Any life is better than no life." Dad won that argument, and he had a point, but I wonder... I could not have lasted a day. Andrew, remarkably, hung in there for over twenty years. He showed incredible courage every day and rarely complained. His bravery was unbelievable.

Before Andrew's accident, Dad had relocated back to England, less than three years after moving his family to Australia. He went back to the UK with a twenty-eight-year-old Australian woman called Sue. Apparently, they got married and stayed in the English countryside for a few years. Dad loved his sports cars and always drove dangerously fast; Mum would always say he never left room on the road for other people to make mistakes. She was right, and consequently, he had quite a few crashes. Dad had a high-speed car accident with Sue and immediately after the crash, Sue wanted to return to Australia. They moved to Sydney and bought a big house on the river, close to the city centre (they were now very wealthy). For a few years, Dad travelled to Adelaide a lot to see Andrew, until finally moving back to Adelaide. Mum bought a small cottage in the hills and lived with a girlfriend. Mum only ever had one man in her life.

The whole family spent a lot of time visiting Andrew. Someone would be there every day to at least try to help and support Ann, because for her it was 24/7. Ann was hard to be around and craved attention. She was in a very challenging and difficult situation; she was doing a great job but was obviously getting frustrated, which made things a tad awkward, complicated, and sometimes unpleasant. I tried to visit only when I knew other people were there.

As the years wore on, it understandably became more difficult for Ann, and she became bitter. She occasionally took her frustrations out on Andrew. Having said that, however, I know that Andrew would not have survived a year without Ann. After a few years, incredibly, they had a son together. This had a hugely positive effect on Andrew. It gave him a reason to persevere and someone to love. Andrew needed all the love he could get and having a baby around gave him a little hope. It was also something else to bring the family together. Whether it was Andrew's child is still not clear, and with all the obvious difficulties, I very much doubt it. If Andrew knew, he never let on; and after he died, Ann cut all ties with us permanently and forbade any contact.

Andrew's story is long, tragic, and complicated. A book called *Oceans of Courage* has been published to tell his unique story. Andrew did go on to recover his voice with the help of Christopher Reeves of *Superman* fame. He studied law, worked on website design, and competed in the world disabled sailing championships. There were 150 competitors. Most of them were paraplegics and therefore had use of their upper body, but Andrew had to steer the boat and control the sails in his racing dinghy, using just his mouth and chin. He finished eighth and won the Disabled Sailor of the Year Award. That took a natural-born skill, determination, and guts!

Andrew chose to end his life about a year later. Ann had moved on, and he was facing the prospect of being institutionalised. Andrew talked to Mum and Dad, and said he was tired and wanted an end to it. Some tried to talk him out of that idea, especially Dad. I can't imagine what it was like for Dad, but he took it badly, as you can imagine. I was not going to try and dissuade Andrew. I felt a sense of relief, for he was my brother, I loved him, and he suffered every day. Andrew arranged all the details. He wasn't like me; he was smart and brave, and he booked a date with death.

When that day arrived, Chris was in America and Mum was too distraught to see him. Liz, Dad, and I went to see Andrew for the last time. We took it in turns to say goodbye. I went into the room and tried to talk, but words would barely come. What on Earth could I possibly say? I was at a loss. It was heartbreaking and we both cried a lot. With great difficulty and after what seemed like an eternity, I told him I was sorry, there was nothing I could do, and I asked him, "Have you thought about what comes next?"

He looked me in the eyes, and this was the last thing he ever said to me: "Yes, I have Si, I'm going home."

We stood by him and stroked his head while the doctor took off the tracheotomy to the machine that pumped air into his lungs. He suffocated. It took about twenty minutes.

It was absolutely harrowing. Andrew really did have oceans of courage; I am, and will always be, in awe of him. I thought it was very fitting that Andrew should make the final call and determine his own fate.

In the end it was tragic, and very special. To be able to talk about death with someone you love, and say goodbye, knowing the exact time they will die, was almost like an execution. I headed home to my family.

Let me share your fear and pain

Walk through fire touched by flame

To the realm of your heart

Bare my soul, take you far

Together defying blood and reason

Thrown before us by gods and demons

Let them march to a different drum

For me the sea and you the sun

So, when darkness falls, we might

Look toward the stars at night

Forever we were always lost

Bold our love

Embrace the cost

Chapter Seven

HAVE YOU GOT A CRIMINAL RECORD?

The musical journey is a road with no destination

You might think the band's first gig would be a party with a small group of friends. That way we could gauge the reaction and get some feedback. But no! Kyle had gone ahead and booked a gig at a local bar, and then forgot to mention it. Out of nowhere we had a couple of weeks to prepare, and we would be on stage for the first time. I named the band Blue Experience. It should have been No Experience!

That was not the first time something like that happened. Kyle would occasionally not show up for hours, or even not show at all. We were great friends, though. Some of his excuses could be hysterical, and the banter and sarcasm over the top.

"Hey, Kyle, what happened yesterday? We were waiting for you all evening."

"Really? I came around earlier and left you a message."

"A message! What message?"

"In the driveway, it was huge. You guys are hopeless, really."

"What do you mean, in the driveway?"

"I got some gravel from the neighbours."

"Gravel? What the fuck?"

"Geezus, mate. I didn't have a pen and paper, so I left a message out of gravel on the driveway. Don't tell me you didn't see it."

"Oh, silly me, next time I'll look for gravel and smoke signals, Morse code even!"

"Look, I saw a girl in a car, so I went to her house."

"Oh, that's all right then. Sorry, mate, I didn't realise you saw a girl in a car."

The day of the gig, we set up early and sound checked. I was nervous and decided to go for a long walk. I had practised a lot, but my energy levels were through the roof and when your energy has nowhere to go, it can turn into nerves. When I got back, we still had an hour or so and I wasn't sure what to do. These days, because I meditate and breathe properly, I can relax and enjoy the experience. Back then as a youngster and with no mentor, I thought, *Fuck it, I know what to do, I'll take a handful of sleeping tablets and drink a bottle of bourbon - that'll take the edge off.*

The place was packed, nothing went horribly wrong, and somehow, we pulled it off. All I had to do was play guitar. It was the mid-eighties, a long time before the internet and mobile phones. One of the most popular forms of entertainment in Australia was live music, the majority of which was made up by good, and even great, bands that wrote and played their own songs, and the pubs, venues, and bars were heaving.

We soon had offers for gigs, but we held off. We did do a house party, because they promised to provide copious amounts of free dope, cocaine, alcohol, mushrooms, and girls. I'm not sure which order it came in. Despite all the drugs, I still remember that gig. We were wild, loud, and crazy. You couldn't spend so much time in the bush, deserts, and ocean without being a rebel, and we tapped into some sort of primal urge. When we hit the stage, we were high energy, slightly aggressive, young and dangerous. All three of us had similar music tastes and we had been genuinely inspired by the great bands of the late '60s and '70s. We dressed and behaved as though we were one of them. We weren't even close, but people loved it and treated us accordingly, especially the girls.

One day I had a surprising phone call from Dad, who asked me to go on a dive trip to the Solomon Islands with him, his wife Sue and their three-year-old son Ben, my half-brother. They needed someone to babysit.

"Sure. Can I bring a girlfriend?"

I invited Sarah, a tall, blond hippy, and, like most hippies, she was from a nice, upper middle-class family. We packed a very small bag and arrived at the airport looking like we had just left Woodstock. We weren't even wearing shoes. As we were approaching the airport at Honiara, I started to get a little apprehensive about the big bag of marijuana I had stuffed down my jeans. I didn't really have a plan, so I transferred it into Dad's briefcase. I felt certain that custom officers would not search a respectable businessman on holiday with his family, even if two of them looked like bloody hippies.

I was wrong, of course! We got off the plane and joined the queue with our passports at the ready. Dad went in front of me, and to my surprise a customs officer stopped Dad and waved the rest of us through. They pulled Dad aside and asked him to open his briefcase. Luckily for all of us, at the last minute I had changed my mind and taken the bag out of his brief case and put it back into my jeans. We walked through the airport, out the front doors and onto the lawn, where we were to wait for another plane. While we waited, I thought it would be a good time to light up a joint, not fifty yards away from the airport entrance. What was I thinking, and how on earth did I not get busted?

We spent a couple of weeks on a small island, diving, surfing, fishing, and looking after Ben, and by sheer good luck, we flew out two days before a massive cyclone tore through the region. It obliterated the island we stayed on, and trapped people in the capital for a month with torrential rain and flooding. On the way back into Australia, it was my turn to get pulled up by customs. The officer was very young and in training, or at least under supervision. He was taking his new job very seriously and with great zeal. He was asking ridiculous questions, insinuating that I must be into drugs, because I had dreadlocks, I was a surfer and musician, living in South Australia, and had a British passport. At the time SA was well known for supplying most of Australia's cannabis, so there was some logic to his assumptions. He had hit the nail on the head, but hey, there was no need to be a knob about it.

After about half an hour, he said, "Sir, do you have a criminal record?"

I replied, "No, I'm sorry, I didn't know you STILL needed one." He didn't seem to appreciate the joke. Fortunately, I had smoked all the weed with the locals on the island and he did not get his first bust!

As soon as I got back into Adelaide, I had a few practice sessions with the band, and we worked on some songs to record, but the ocean was always calling. I took off for the west coast. I usually slept in my car and made do with the bare minimum - something to cook with, my surfing and diving gear and some food and water. If I hit a kangaroo with the car, which wasn't out of the ordinary, I would take it down the beach, clean, gut and skin it. Then I would cook it in a fire pit and share it with whoever was around.

Meanwhile, my friend Zac was still living in a small fishing village with his girlfriend. Apart from working the fishing boats, Zac had started hunting for fox tails as he could get about 30 dollars for each tail. I was catching a lift back to camp with him and his girlfriend Cindy, when he saw a fox on the side of the road. It had just been hit by a car, or so he thought!

"Wait here, you guys. I won't be long - that looks like thirty dollars right there." He got out of the car and said, "Easy money." He swaggered over, pulled out a ridiculously big hunting knife, put his foot on the body of the fox, and it exploded. We could hear a giant farting noise from the car forty feet away, and before he could jump back, it sprayed him with putrid fluid. It had been dead for ages and had bloated in the forty-degree sun, and as soon as he even touched it, bang, it went off like a bomb. We absolutely fell about laughing. Zac started gagging, which made us laugh even more. But it was disgusting and unfortunately for us, all he had in the car for cleaning were a couple of pages from an old newspaper. The smell was rank and powerful.

Through all the laughing, Cindy said, "Oh yeah, easy money, eh."

"Shut up, you're gunna have to put up with the stench too. Bloody fucking fox, fuck."

I couldn't pass up the opportunity. "Fucking hell, mate, you smell worse than you did before. Get driving and open the bloody windows, quick."

Zac drove in silence all the way back, while I made up a little song called "Easy Money".

About a year earlier, I was with Zac when a few of us were camping on a remote headland near a great reef break. It was late at night when we heard Zac shouting for us to come and check out a miracle, and we all got up and found him standing in the dark, fifty feet away.

"What the fuck, Zac! Where's this miracle?" He looked so pleased with himself. He turned on a torch and pointed it at the ground.

"Check that out. If that's not a world record, I don't know what is."

Bob, standing next to me said, "I don't believe it. Is that even real?"

There were gasps of disbelief and murmurings of "oh my God". I looked down and to my horror, saw a six-foot-long giant turd. Zac was like a proud father.

"Yeah, look at that. I had to shuffle along as it came out, so it didn't back up and break. That's got to be a world record. Look, I'll show you how I-"

Bob cut him off. "No, no, no. It's fine. We don't need to see any more. You're very talented, congratulations, now I'm going back to sleep, probably to have nightmares."

The next morning, we were woken by Zac excitedly shouting for us to come and look again. I was morning grumpy and getting annoyed. We all walked over to see him standing there with a stupid, slightly shocked look on his face.

I said, "What the fuck, Zac?"

"Look," he pointed to the ground. "It's gone!" It had gone. The whole giant turd had disappeared, just like that, all six feet of it!

It was another friend, whom we called Bear, who said, "Do you think it ran off?"

"Probably not," Bob said, with just a hint of sarcasm. "I think it's been eaten!" Bob was the clever one with a university degree in Zoology. He had a big grin on his face as he turned to me.

And I said, "Well, don't look at me, mate!"

We moved camp, just in case there was a giant turd-eating monster on the prowl.

I was starting to feel torn between two worlds. One was freedom and an almost idyllic surfing lifestyle, and the other was perhaps the more complicated but interesting life of a young musician in the city. I eventually rented a house in the city centre with my band mates. It was one extreme to another, again!

The band rehearsed often and recorded an EP. We started to get a decent amount of airplay on a few of Adelaide's radio stations, including SAFM, Adelaide's biggest mainstream FM station. We rode a wave of popularity and started performing two or three nights a week. One show at a well-known venue called the Tivoli was particularly crowded, and we had just finished on a high when we were approached by a guy called Lenny.

"Hey, you guys are great, love the energy. How about I book a few gigs for you and if it goes well, I could manage things for you."

"Yeah, sure," I said, without thinking to ask any questions.

"I want you to meet a friend of mine," he said. "He's a phenomenal drummer. Trust me, he will blow you away. I'll call and arrange for you to meet."

I met Nui later that night. He approached me at a bar in the early hours of the morning.

"Hey man, great gig. I like what you're doing. It's wild."

"Thanks, mate. Are you Lenny's friend?"

"Yeah man, I'm Nui. I'm a drummer, been playing since I was four years old." "About ten years then," I said, with a smile. I thought he was going to punch me.

He was very intoxicated, but he just grinned and said, "No man, and you need me. You should put Kyle out the front singing and I'll play drums for you. It'll be great,"

"Okay. Everything's set up at our place for jamming. Come around tomorrow night."

Nui showed up the next day, with a suitcase, and stayed. He was a few years older than us, vastly more experienced, and musically he was on another level. He was a phenomenal drummer and incredibly talented. He was so good that a few days later, he was called away to tour with the Doobie Brothers. They were touring Australia and their drummer had flown home sick. A couple of weeks later, I came home one night, and Nui was back, which would have been great except he was asleep in my bed and wearing my clothes. He was a real vagabond who owned nothing and was just as wild as the rest of us. He was a naturally gifted all-round musician, but he also had some mental health issues. His more pressing problem, however, was that an outlaw motorcycle gang wanted him dead. In fact, there were several people who wanted to kill him, as we would soon find out.

On the plus side, he transformed the band overnight with his brilliance. He brought an intoxicating energy, and with his powerful drumming and technique, created a heap of space in the songs for innovation and improvisation. One night, the David Lee Roth band were in town with Steve Vai and other luminaries. We got word they were going to a pub where one of our friends was playing, and I went along. By this stage Nui was following me around everywhere, and I mean everywhere, which was getting slightly annoying. He would borrow money, wear my clothes, take my car, and when he wanted to go out thieving, take my dogs.

Anyway, back to the gig with the American super stars. The drummer from The David Lee Roth band played the last song with our friends' band and finished the song with a big drum solo. Now, Nui was waiting around the corner for his chance and pushed his way past the security guys and jumped on the kit. Without saying a word, he started to play a drum solo, the likes of which I doubt many people have ever heard. He played like a man possessed, but he also had the technique and ability. Everyone watched in awe. He played so fast and powerfully that it looked as though he had levitated off the seat. He had an explosive energy, both feet kicking with speed and precision whilst he simultaneously attacked the snare and rolled around the tom toms. It filled the room with an amazing sound and as he finished playing, the whole place burst into rapturous applause. Nui just got up, and without acknowledging anyone, he left.

Nui was unpredictable and, I think, a bit disappointed, frustrated, and bitter that he hadn't made it. He certainly had the talent and experience to achieve great things, but he, like myself, had his demons, and he liked the booze and drugs way too much.

The band grew in popularity, and we developed a strong following, albeit a short-lived one. We started a residency at a venue called The Century on Adelaide's one and only main drag. It was right alongside some of the less reputable venues, bars and strip clubs, and in the mid to late '80s, it became one of Australia's most notorious hotels, for good reason. Things were about to get crazy!

The eternal watcher looks through you

Like a flower needs the sun

In the desert

In the rain

Hands open

Smile on your face

Through the darkness

Death is mine

You're a witness

Love divine

Can't be hurt

Can't be wrong

Oh so silent

So strong

The story of life is the story of love

It's so obscene

You take a gun

Sorrow and pain

I knew I'd find

With love I feel

That's so sublime

Are you the warrior or the cheat

In the mirror

The truth you seek

No past no future too

Only what lies inside of you.

Chapter Eight

LIGHT MY FIRE

A good argument can only be had by agreement

The Century Hotel was so bad, it was good. Why? Well, for a start, the place was always overcrowded. It stayed open until the sun came up. It was dirty, smelly, hot, dark, and gloomy. There was constant fighting, drugs, prostitution, and underage girls, and that would be a Monday morning. It also hosted a plethora of original rock bands seven nights a week. The staff and security were as troublesome and out-of-control as the highly intoxicated patrons, plus the owner was part of an Eastern European crime gang. It was like the wild west, except it was the mid-'8os in Adelaide.

The owner was a devious, cunning, and highly unethical man called Roland, who had his fingers in as many pies as possible, most of them illegal. He had fourteen children, and in a strange way was quite likable. He was also the most atrocious driver I have ever known. He wouldn't look behind him when reversing, well, at least not properly, and he would just smash into everything, a car, fence, traffic light, whatever. He also drove completely shit-faced, blind drunk, stoned, and with an attitude that said the speed limit was "Go as fast as you can, at all times!" He did eventually die behind the wheel in a high-speed car chase, trying to evade other criminals.

We gigged at his hotel almost every week, and over the years I got to know him well. We started a distribution business together. I would sell my bush crops to him, and he would hire a plane and have people fly it around Australia. I spent a substantial amount of time at the hotel or at his mansion. I'd go around to his house occasionally in the late afternoons, and he would always be in bed half asleep with the TV on, usually the cricket. He wasn't exactly a picture of good health.

He said to me once as I stood in the doorway of his bedroom, "You know why I like the cricket so much?"

"Not really, mate."

He had a big grin on his face, underneath his big scruffy beard. "Well, you can fall asleep for hours, wake up and you haven't missed anything." Geoffrey Boycott must have been batting!

I found out later that he used to test people's honesty by leaving a bag of cocaine out on the table. He would leave it open and in full view of his visitor. He did this to me on one occasion. He would make an excuse and leave the room. He had a sophisticated set-up of hidden cameras and would watch from another room before coming back in. Luckily for me, it was a test I passed.

These days my band might play six or seven gigs a year. Back in the eighties, it was up to four gigs a week. We travelled vast distances, sometimes doing two shows a night, and we were paid well. The music scene in Adelaide was thriving. The pubs, clubs and venues were packed to the rafters, including the universities.

It was chaotic in the band's share house. There were all sorts of people coming and going, and constant parties, drugs, drinking and girls, girls, girls. I had the back of the house, which I had converted into a lounge and bedroom. I had three Rottweilers and spent a vast amount of time training and looking after them. I would take them through the city parklands late at night, and they came everywhere with me. They were obedient, protective, and fierce. I think the greatest of all sins is betrayal, and they were loyal.

Another venue on the main drag was The Royal Admiral, where the owner liked the band because we were pulling crowds. I had finished one gig there by shoving my guitar through the ceiling and leaving it wedged up to the body, screaming feedback as we walked offstage. The following gig at that venue, I tried to top that finale with something a little more extravagant and it didn't end well, although it was entertaining.

I had brought in some flammable liquid. Unlike Hendrix, who famously used lighter fluid to torch his guitar at the Monterrey pop festival, I thought I would use petrol - lighter fluid was for pussies! As we ended our last song of the night, I poured the whole bottle of petrol over the guitar and thought I'd leave the guitar over my shoulder and keep playing for as long as possible.

However, I had splashed petrol all over my clothes. I leant down into the crowd and a young guy used his lighter to fire up the guitar. It burst into flames. I threw the guitar down, but my clothes had caught fire. I looked at the crowd and they stared at me, as though it was all part of a bizarre show. I tried to put the flames out with my hands, but it didn't work. I fell to the floor and started rolling around, and that seemed to work, until I stood up, whereupon I turned into a human fire ball. Thankfully, my quick-thinking drummer (yes, I know, that's an oxymoron) ripped the stage curtains down and bowled me over, then wrapped me up and suffocated the flames. I went out the fire exit, ironically, and peeled my clothes off. Someone arrived with ice and I tried to cool the burns as best I could for the next half hour or so.

I was badly burnt, especially my right leg, and I was too embarrassed to go to hospital. I did go the next day, however, as I needed painkillers. I told the doctor and staff some bull-shit story about spilling petrol on my leg when I was repairing a lawnmower, but they didn't believe me, especially as one of the doctors said it looked like I'd had a blowtorch held to my leg. I had third degree burns the size of a dinner plate on my thigh and burns to the side of my body, arms, and hand. I had a nurse come to the house every day for a few weeks to change the dressings, and I was laid up for a couple of months.

We recorded another EP onto tape while I still had bandages, and the pain only made me play with more focus and feeling. I wrote all the songs, played guitar, and did all the vocals. It received great reviews and airplay, including some commercial radio stations. Our popularity grew.

We did another tour, this time down the southeast, and the cracks started to appear. For a couple of years, we had been one of the most exciting and popular bands in SA, but there were always distractions. The first gig of the tour, Nui and Kyle missed sound check and disappeared to knock off a bag of speed and a carton of beer. By the time we went on stage, they were completely wasted and couldn't get it together. To make things worse, we had a Spinal Tap moment when Kyle, spinning his mic stand through the air, brought the legs down on my head, almost knocking me out. The old mic stands have a heavy weight at the bottom of the stand to keep them stable, and that hit me dead centre.

The last gig, however, was a sell-out and we played like a well-oiled machine. We were sitting around after the show enjoying a drink when the manager of the venue and his security staff decided they didn't like us. Lenny, who was managing the band, was pumped up on amphetamines, and whenever Lenny consumed speed, the result would be him talking so fast that no-one could understand a word he said. They refused to pay up. After a very intense stand-off, which included a heck of a lot of posturing, pacing, shouting and death threats, I managed to calm things down enough for us to get back to our rooms in one piece. We hung out until the sun came up and things got a bit crazy. There may have been a little bit of damage done to the rooms. We hit the road. It was a very country sort of town, they thought we were freaks and we thought they were freaks. We didn't go back, EVER! I really didn't want to see a band mate squealing like a pig!

There was a new venue in town, and as was often the case, it did not last long. Sometimes a venue would pop up, get trashed, and close, but for a while the Botanic was a cool little place to gig; it was downstairs in the basement with a great atmosphere and good acoustics. Our first gig there was very memorable, but for the wrong reasons. We had a great crowd, and the place was rocking early. It looked like it was going to be a good night. As we went on stage, I noticed two good-looking girls in their early twenties down the front. They were a little tipsy, drinking, dancing, and singing along to the house music. I forgot about them as we started the show.

Halfway through the first set, with my eyes closed and leaning back into another way-too-long guitar solo, I realised someone was spraying me in the face with a warm liquid. I opened my eyes to see that the two girls I'd noticed earlier had taken their tops off and were vigorously squeezing their breasts, taking it in turns to walk up and down the stage in front of the band, spraying us with breast milk! I was amazed. I didn't even know you could do that! I very cleverly deduced that they must have been breastfeeding mothers who had left their babies at home, and like all good mums, decided they were going to go out and get hammered. It was something! I mean, it was the only time I can remember that the band completely stopped playing mid-song. Meanwhile, the girls turned on the crowd and it got very rowdy. Eventually security arrived and took them away, probably to get their phone numbers. Lucky bastards!

I met a girl. She was good-looking, young, blonde, and dangerous. Her name was Joni. I still don't understand why, but she nearly killed me on three occasions, and I don't mean by accident. I wasn't so easy to kill, as it turned out, mainly because I was my own worst enemy and no-one else could come close. I mean to say, good people, that on some mornings my brunch would consist of dope and hashish, cocaine, speed, heroin, and perhaps some LSD or magic mushrooms, all lovingly washed down with a bottle of bourbon. As you can imagine, I had developed a significant tolerance to drugs and alcohol. It was obviously just an overt form of self-harm, especially once I started using heroin. I had already overdosed too many times to count. I'd often be hanging on for dear life and manage to revive myself with water, lying under a running tap on someone's front lawn, or crawling into a bathtub, pool, dam, or the best medicine of all, the ocean. Water was my saviour, and it saved my life many times.

The situation with Joni was bizarre and it caught me off guard, especially as she seemed to like me. I had split with a girlfriend and had just started dating another girl, who lived on the other side of town. I was, in Joni's reasoning, very much fair game. She brought a girlfriend of hers to the house one day and they came into my bedroom, sat on the bed and pulled out a bag of heroin.

"Do you want a taste?"

"Sure," I said, slightly hesitantly. I was still a little wary of using smack, especially if I didn't know where it came from, as I knew the wrong dose could kill you. It had recently killed two friends; they were found in a car, and neither of them had even had time to remove the syringe.

Joni shared it out and I noticed that one of the portions was at least twice the size of the others. At the same time I got distracted by Joni taking her top off and kissing me. She whispered in my ear, "Lie down. Relax, babe, let me hit you up." That sentence is embarrassing. It's hard to even think about, let alone write, I'm cringeing so much. I'm going to stop for a bit, make a cup o' tea, go for a walk, meditate, and do some breathing exercises, whilst repeating, "I am not the body, I am not the mind!"

She hit me up, all right. I knew I was in trouble pretty much straight away, especially when I saw her and the friend put on their clothes, pick up their bags and leave. I had been given a hot shot and the room was spinning. It was horrendous. Colour dissolved into black and white, and I knew if I didn't get up right away, I may never get up. I didn't want to die, especially like that. I pulled myself together and staggered down the hallway, holding onto the wall and vomiting along the way. I made it outside into the cold air, hoping to find some help, and coincidentally Tim showed up just when I really needed him, as a great friend can do from time to time. He helped me, fully clothed, into an ice-cold shower and there I sat, under the water, fighting to stay conscious. After hanging on by the skin of my teeth for what seemed like an eternity, I crawled into bed and passed out.

The second incident with the she-devil was at a party after a gig. I had taken a couple of Rohypnol and washed them down with a bottle of bourbon. Late into the party, I crashed in someone's bed. Joni arrived, came into the bedroom, and woke me up, supposedly to make sure I was okay!

"Simon, take some of these, they'll make you feel better. Here, just take a few."

"Okay, thanks. How many are there?"

"Just finish them; there's only about ten. They're not very strong."

I was half-conscious and completely out of it, so down the hatch they went! I grabbed a bottle of wine and after a few minutes started to feel better. We left the party and hopped into her van, which of course had a nice big, fat bed in the back. We drove to another party.

Days later, I was told by a reliable witness that I had taken about a dozen 10mg Valium tablets and was completely out of control. I had gotten into a fight with every other guy at the party and been beaten up and thrown out - not for the first time, I might add. I don't remember much, but I do remember copping a beating. We left the scene and Joni pulled over in a suburban street to have sex in her van. At that stage something strange, dark, and primal possessed me. I literally turned into a wild beast! I tore our clothes off and we had some sort of violent and weird sex. I woke up at about 5am at her parents' house, miles down the south coast. I got out of bed and put on what was left of my clothes, and Joni woke up.

"Where are you going?"

"Home."

"Wait, I can give you a lift."

"No thanks."

Half-dressed, I staggered out of the house in a daze. I ran into the street, put my head down and kept running. About four hours later I made it home. Joni showed up on my doorstep a few hours later, having thoughtfully decided to return my underpants which, I might add, looked very much like they had seen better days.

My third encounter was at another party, and again I arrived a little tipsy (I had drunk only one bottle of bourbon this time). As I walked up the driveway I was met by Joni. She put her arms around me, kissed me, and led me into the party, next to a large pool. She suggested a swim and I was too out of it to suggest that it may not be a good idea. I sat down on the ground next to the pool and started to take my jeans off. What I didn't know was that Joni now had a boyfriend, and as I sat on the ground, he came up behind me and kicked me in the side of the head. I was stunned and he attacked me, punching me in the head over and over in a violent rage. Eventually, while some people dragged him off, I fell unconscious. This had to be explained to me after the event by other party-goers who had witnessed the attack.

I think the same people carried me to a bedroom, and I came around a few minutes later as Joni was having sex with me while her boyfriend sulked in his car. She was psycho, and perhaps I was too! About an hour later, I left the party and her boyfriend attacked me again. This time, I was sober, and I fought back like an animal. The police arrived, so I jumped a fence and legged it. I have not seen Joni since. We were quite the couple!

The stranger on a stage

Looks at the serpent's head

Ink-stained fingers, blood-soaked hands

Conceived and lost without a plan

So, here's a prison,

I made your mind

With tales of misery

I dreamed of time in a sea of stars

And left a mystery!

So, reach up

As far as you can and heal the broken man

You loved and lost and loved again

The clues beneath the sand

It's dark, it's cruel and lost forever

look toward the sun

Another breath, a beating heart

The stones inside a ring

The earth looks up

The sky falls down

Just let the angels sing.

Chapter Nine

POLICE WITH SHOTGUNS

Look back to see the way ahead

My band disintegrated again. They always did. No-one got paid much, if anything, and we usually spent what we earned on recording. Everyone had stuff going on and unless you had some success, people get fed up and leave. Who could blame them? It was a lot of work and commitment with little or no return.

Nui had always showed up to the gigs drunk and out of it, but it was getting out of control. He was always getting into fights, causing trouble, and sometimes showing up with serious criminals. I kicked him out of the house and the band fell apart. A few weeks later, Eddie and I started the band up again as a three-piece, with a young guy on drums whose nickname was Fee Color. However, we were never going to be able to replace Nui. He was a force of nature, and the band was not as good without him. Just like that, our popularity vanished. Gone!

Nui would occasionally come to the house and his behaviour was erratic. He took my dogs to a dodgy drug deal, stole my car twice and got pulled over by the police both times. I only found out because, ironically, the police pulled me over one night and told me all about his late-night adventures in my car, and why they had a warrant for his arrest. The final straw, however, was two guys rocking up at the house, forcing their way in with a handgun, and pointing it at the poor sod who just so happened to answer the door. Nui had ripped them off and they wanted blood. I never saw Nui again after that night. I heard he headed for the Northern Territory.

One night, on the way home, with a car full of girls wanting to party, I passed a patrol car that had pulled over on the other side of the road. It was very early morning, and everyone was high and/or drunk. We were about a mile or so from home, and as we drove past, I looked over to see the police checking us out. I kept an eye on them in the side mirror as we headed up the road, but I already knew what was going to happen.

"Here we go. Hang on, I reckon we can make it."

The police put the lights on, pulled a U-turn and came after us at high speed. I knew the area well, so I floored it and turned off the main road. I did a couple of left turns, right turns, and went down an alley. We flew around the last corner sideways, and I killed the lights and sped up the road to the house. In my mirror, I saw the police fly through the intersection and miss our street. I pulled over, using the hand brake to stop so the brake lights wouldn't come on. Everybody piled out of the car and headed for the house, but the door was locked. Someone noticed a front window open and started climbing in. Everyone followed, falling over each other and laughing. As the captain is the last one off his sinking ship, I was the last one through the window, just as the cops arrived. After that, the only problem was trying to stop everyone from giggling as we sat in the dark and watched the police searching up and down the street.

The new band headed out to the Yorke Peninsula, and we stayed in a shack on the beach for an extended and much-needed practice. One night, very late, I got into a fight with my ex-girlfriend's new fella, and it got a bit loud. I threw a thick glass jug at the outside wall, and it went off with a loud bang. However, it did not sound like I had shot someone, which was reported to the police about fifty miles away. A couple of hours later, I woke up to the dogs going crazy, I looked out the window to see two policemen running down the driveway holding shotguns. I called the dogs off and ran around the house stashing all the drugs, including some rather large bags of marijuana. Suzie and Andrea were asleep on the couch, and I was in a rush. I lifted their pillows and shoved the bags under. They did look a little surprised.

I just said, "It's the cops. Whatever happens, pretend to be asleep, don't speak and try not to move." I looked up just as the door flew open and two cops ran in.

"Geezus, you got pump action shotguns!" One of them tripped over the doorstep on the way in and I half expected to get blown in two. I was standing there in my boxers.

"Fucking hell, guys, what's the problem?" I was trying to not sound aggressive, seeing as they were both pointing guns in my direction, and I suspect at least one of them fancied himself as Clint Eastwood. He could speak and everything.

"We got a call you shot someone."

"What the fuck? Who called? I don't own a gun. For Christ's sake, there are no guns here. You've been here before - you know me!"

Mr Eastwood spoke again. It was amazing. "Stay where you are and don't move. We're gunna look around."

One of them stayed with me in the main room, watched by several people in sleeping bags all not daring to move. The other police officer (it's "officer" when they're holding a shotgun) looked around. They left a few minutes later, empty-handed, and now missing a heap of police equipment like handcuffs, torches, walkie-talkies and breath analysers, as my friend and neighbour, LZ, had noticed the commotion, run over, climbed into their van, and helped himself, cheeky bugger!

We spent the next few days hanging out and jamming, then we headed back to the big smoke. We had to start again. We had lost the crowd, and the music scene was always changing and evolving. We were not the same band, and we were now playing empty rooms. People move on; it was tough.

It got worse! I broke my middle finger badly, and it was on my left hand, which I used to fret the guitar. I had played a gig with it broken the night it happened - not a good idea. I started to lose confidence. I had an operation, but it took a long time to heal and once it had healed, I couldn't bend it, and still can't today. A few years later I badly broke my little finger on the same hand, which is not exactly ideal for a guitarist.

On top of that, I split with another girlfriend, and I didn't take it well. I was a wreck and dealt with it badly. I tried to numb the pain with even more drugs and alcohol. I realise now that the pain I buried when Dad left, and the pain I felt for Andrew, kept rearing its ugly head, and all because I wouldn't deal with the situation in the first place. I just buried it and let it fester.

I started hanging around with a girl called Deb, who was just as messed up as I was. We spent the next few weeks encouraging and supporting each other to get as wasted, miserable and dysfunctional as possible, and without ever having a decent conversation, or even sex, for that matter.

We always went out late, and one weekend we headed into the city looking for trouble. We ended up on the main strip, behind a very large and expensive muscle car with personalised number plates. It was full of young men who objected to me being too close behind them, and they appeared to not like my car. They leant out of the windows to shout abuse and Deb retaliated with some very colourful and not so eloquent language, something she seemed to excel in. A couple of them jumped out of the car and threatened us. They shouldn't have done that!

They pulled around a corner, just off the main street, and I pulled over in front of them. We let a friend get out of the car; she had been sitting in the back seat looking slightly terrified. Deb and I should have driven off, but we got out of the car. We didn't care that half a dozen aggressive men had already taken offence at us being there, not to mention all the abuse that had been flying back and forth. They got out and walked over. A couple of them ran up the street, reappearing a few minutes later with friends, otherwise known as reinforcements. Next thing we knew, there were about a dozen of them, and they were itching for a fight.

I turned to Deb and said, "Look, there's heaps of them and only two of us. No offence or anything, but one of us is a girl. Let's go."

She tended to ignore everything I said from that point on. "You guys can fuck off. You're all a bunch of fags anyway."

I was thinking, *Ooh, I wonder if she'll marry me. She'd make a great mum.* Actually, it was more like, *Shit, here we go.*

"Deb, get in the car before they beat the crap out of us."

She just pushed me away and I turned around to face them, shrugging my shoulders. I had my back against the car. They were in a tight semi-circle, within punching distance, and they didn't look happy. I suddenly thought it was all very funny and started laughing. I even apologised.

"Sorry about that, she's a bit upset."

One of them, who was in the centre of the group, punched me hard in the face. I just grinned at him and went into a rant about everything and nothing. They looked a bit confused. I had become friendly and started to chat. It didn't last long though, as Deb started up again.

"What are you fucking looking at? Why don't you fuck off?"

That set them off. One of them pushed her up against the car. "Shut your mouth, bitch, or I'll shut it for you."

I stepped in, pushed him away, and as the punches rained down on my head, I looked up without even trying to protect myself.

"You bunch of fucking pussies."

It didn't take long before I felt drained of energy. It was a type of tired I hadn't felt before, as though I just wanted to go to sleep and not wake up. It was strange. Time appeared to slow down almost to a standstill, and I felt detached, as if I was in a meditation. I sobered up quickly and, better late than never, had a moment of clarity. No more feeling sorry for myself! Deb was as drunk and suicidal as I was, so I had to forcefully push her into the car while taking blows to the head. I jumped in next to her and noticed I was bleeding badly. I kept them at bay just long enough to shut the door and start the car.

I dropped it into gear and floored it. I was about a hundred yards up the street, when I slammed on the brakes. I don't know where the idea came from, and I didn't give it a second thought. I popped it into reverse and floored it again, smoking up the tyres at high speed; and with my foot to the floor. I drove my beat-up van with its big old, nasty tow bar straight into their expensive street machine. There was a hell of an impact. The front of their car disintegrated. It was a write-off. I smoked up the tyres again, this time with Deb hanging out the window, whooping and hollering. Surprisingly, no-one got my number plate, I didn't kill anyone, and I didn't get arrested. You see, there is a God, and that night, she was on my side!

My good friend and bass player left the band next. He had girlfriend problems. I replaced him with a talented young man called Dominic, who was a brilliant bass player but suffered from schizophrenia. He came from a very wealthy family with a strange and slightly scary mother who had a habit of jumping out of the bushes every time I went over to the family home to pick him up. She was a real handful, and so was Dominic. Halfway through a gig he would disappear, and I'd usually find him gazing into a television as if he'd never seen one before; or he'd be hiding in a corner, eating chocolate biscuits he'd stolen.

One morning at about 3am, I was dropping him home from a gig and speeding up Magill Road with a van full of band equipment, including a hefty old PA system. Dominic, as usual, started to complain that he was hungry, which was fair enough, as he hadn't eaten for at least fifteen minutes! It was getting annoying, so I thought I'd freak him out, which was relatively easy to do. I sped up. We were just about to go hurtling through the traffic lights at a cross intersection, when at the last second, I swerved into the turn-left-only lane, hoping to make the fast-food joint.

The problem was, I hadn't seen the concrete median strip in the middle of the road. Half a second before impact, Dominic let out a high-pitched scream that sounded like an eight-year-old girl in a horror movie. We took out a rather large road sign and then hit the concrete strip, which acted like a ramp, launching the van into the air at high speed. We cleared two lanes in one jump. When we landed, the impact was something else. The noise of all the band equipment crashing around in the back was deafening, and the suspension snapped with such bone-crunching force, I thought my teeth were going to fall out. Somehow, we missed all the other road users, and no police were called, again! We both turned to look at each other, as if to say, "Wow, we're still alive. Let's not do that again!"

In a rather high-pitched and squeaky little voice, Dominic said, "Back in a minute. I'll just get a sausage roll!"

In The Hearts of Men

Sunsets running lines of gold
On silver water the air turns cold
A ship sails by on a thousand dreams
A star is born
A little girl sleeps
The star shines softly bold and bright
A young man tries to make things right

You know
I can't believe my eyes
This time I realise
How do you feel when you're on your own?
How do you feel when you're all alone?
How do you feel?

Now innocence and virtue meet
Like gentle streams beneath your feet
A mother cries
A father weeps
They hold each other and fall asleep
In their dreams
They see a child
When they awake
Embrace and smile

You know
I can't believe my eyes
It's time to make things right
This time is right
The time is right
How do you feel when you're on your own?
How do you feel when you're all alone?
How do you feel?

Chapter Ten

DEEP IN SOUL

My soul is no coward
Through the tempest I have walked
Laid my fate at the door
In the heart of the storm

Deep in Soul is a song I wrote in 1995. It was recorded by Mick at Mix Masters in Adelaide, as a duet with Tania. Her partner Ross was a friend who repaired and maintained all my music equipment. He is an electronics whiz and makes custom guitar amplifiers and all things valve. Tania has a beautiful voice, and it worked.

Meanwhile, the band had gone through at least half a dozen drummers and more than half a dozen bass players. Because of that, the band's sound was always changing and evolving.

We now had Kylena, a young woman doing backing vocals. I also brought Taz in to play keys and synth. He was an excellent musician with classical training. I had a great new bass player called Adrian, who went on to become a high-profile lawyer. However, he didn't stay long and was eventually replaced by a keen surfer and top bloke from NSW called Chris, and finally, Shane on drums. He was a good young player who looked like he'd been born in the Shire next door to Bilbo. My songwriting had improved and what we lacked with the departure of Nui, we made up for with originality and diversity. The new band released an album, and lo and behold, EMI came calling. However, I will come to that shortly (I hope you don't mind me calling you shortly). Anyway, something even more important than EMI was about to happen.

I met the love of my life! Kylea was just sixteen, but for me it was love at first sight. Corny but true! I waited a few days and then called to arrange a date. I met her at the Flinders Uni bar, as it was next door to the hospital where her mum was having a baby. That was about thirty years ago and yes, we are still together. I knew I had found the woman I wanted to be with. She had dark curly hair, a petite curvy figure, stunning green eyes and a beautiful smile. She was also a great dancer, smart and confident. It was never going to be easy, however, as I was twenty-eight and Kylea was sixteen, which meant her friends and peers were sixteen. Kylea was ten years older than her next sibling and there were four other siblings, so her mum was preoccupied with kids and babies. Kylea had become the wild child and she usually did what she wanted when she wanted.

It wasn't long before she moved out of home and into a share house with Jo, a woman in her early thirties, who ironically was a youth worker. Kylea would sometimes stay over at my place, which I shared with two other musicians, especially on weekends when we were gigging and hanging out with friends. One night at Kylea's place, there was an incident with my three Rottweilers. Things got ugly when a very drunk and aggressive ex-boyfriend of Jo's showed up. Trouble was, Jo didn't want anything to do with the ex-boyfriend and she wouldn't open the door. He decided to go around the back and jump the gate. I ran around and started shouting at him over and over to back off, while I held the dogs back; but of course, he was so intoxicated he wouldn't listen. Every time he climbed onto the gate, I would wrestle with him and push him back.

The dogs went crazy, lunging, snarling, and trying to bite him. They were well trained, but Marshall hated drunk people, and as soon as they could smell alcohol, there was potential for someone to get bitten. After a while he made it past me and jumped over. He did of course get bitten on the hand, and the arm, and I suppose now is an opportune time to mention a slightly nasty bite on the leg as well. But hey - at least he didn't die. And he did finally wander off up the street, albeit bleeding pretty badly and missing half a leg! We grabbed some of Kylea's things, put the dogs in the car, and took off for an extended holiday up the east coast, just before the police arrived.

After a few weeks we were back, and I arranged the band to go into the hills for a week and record an album at Mix

Masters studio; it was called *Future Traditions* and was an eclectic mix of psychedelic and blues rock. The album received great reviews in the local papers and street magazines, and I booked a tour of the east coast to help promote and sell the album.

The tours were difficult to organise but were good fun. We would hire a large van and trailer and pile in, including girlfriends and sound crew. We would camp on the long slow drives over and get accommodation at the pubs where we played. It's quite a few thousand miles there and back, so we would usually be away for a few weeks. We had a few ups and downs, hits and misses, but generally the gigs were packed and rocking. We toured several times without any major arguments or fallout.

I set fire to the bus on one occasion (well, two occasions really) but at least no-one got seriously injured. How does one set fire to a bus? Well, as it turns out, it is relatively easy if you're smoking bongs in the back of a very cramped bus for hours and hours and there's a heap of hessian cloth and other flammable material. I was too stoned to notice at first, but somehow the hessian cloth caught alight just behind me and the bus started to fill with smoke.

"Is it just me or is it getting a big smoky in here?" We pulled over on the side of the road. It must have looked like a Cheech and Chong film as we staggered out of the bus fanning the smoke away, coughing and falling about laughing.

I had always hidden my hard drug use from everybody, but it was starting to catch up with me. It was expensive and exhausting, especially trying to hide the sickness when I would inevitably start going into withdrawals. I didn't talk to Kylea about it, and she didn't know. It was hard work, debilitating, depressing and stressful. I was living a lie.

We moved again, this time into a beach house, and Kylea and I agreed to share with two or three of her friends. At first it was fun, especially being down at the beach again. We were playing gigs every week, avoiding responsibility – damn the consequences. We were there about a year or so before we moved again. Two of the girls we house shared with were on the same motorbike when they had a nasty accident, at night, with no headlights and no brakes! ("Didn't see that coming!") They were hospitalised and later went back to their families. Kylea and I moved further down the south coast to a small beachside town.

My dogs were about ten years old by then and I took them to the vet to be put down. Marshall had deteriorated after a stroke and Gemma had cancer. I was devastated. I still had no idea how to deal with emotional pain, so I took some pills, got drunk, and stuck a broken bottle in my arm, as you do. Without really meaning to, I had made a seriously deep cut down to the bone, tearing through some major veins, and it bled heavily. Kylea was out studying at the time and came home hours later to find me just as I was passing out. She called an ambulance, but some friends showed up and took me to hospital. No-one thought to cancel the ambulance! When they arrived and no-one answered the door, they called the police, who kicked the front door in. Trouble was, there were large pools of blood in the kitchen and bathroom, and all my cannabis plants drying in the bedroom, lounge, hallway, spare room, pantry and shed. Whoops!

So please, do us a favour here and go back to the prologue. Don't tut, it's easy. Turn the pages over. Saves me writing it all over. I'm thinking of the environment - we are saving paper. While you're at it, be a dear and make us a cup o' tea.

Welcome back, right, so there we are, me and Kylea just arrived in Bali. We are in Denpasar Airport, and I am about to get busted with a few grams of heroin and a dozen methadone tablets, so was probably going to rot in a smelly, sweaty, filthy jail cell while I waited for a date with the firing squad. I can just imagine it. "Does the prisoner have any last words?" Shit yeah, how about, "Hold your fire!"

It wasn't as if I had smuggled in drugs to profit off someone else's misery. No, I had turned making my own life a misery into an art form. I had taken enough drugs with me to stop myself from going into withdrawals; it wouldn't have been much of a holiday, especially for Kylea, if I had started frothing at the mouth, vomiting, and dealing with explosive diarrhoea. Actually, that sounds like a normal day in Bali. Anyway, you get my point. Kylea didn't know, and I wasn't ready to tell her. No-one knew. I was continually dealing with what was immediately in front of me and hoping for the best. So, this policemen with his sniffer dog walks straight towards me. The dog looks young - I think it's a Beagle; I love dogs, just not ones that send you to the gallows. They were half a dozen paces away when I abruptly stepped out of line, taking the policemen and his dog by surprise. I swiftly knelt as if to pat the dog, but instead I grabbed him and rolled him over onto his back.

"Who's a good boy who likes his tummy being rubbed?" I was talking to the dog.

"Hey, leave the dog alone. Don't touch the dog!" Jeez, he was shouting and looked angry. I feigned surprise, as if I was a bit thick (so I was basically just being myself). Anyway, the officer yanked hard on the lead and pulled the dog up and over. He looked embarrassed and stormed off in a huff. Scheisse, that were close, good doggy!

The truly mind-blowing thing, now I look back on it, was that I wasn't particularly nervous. The next year, we went back for Christmas, I did it again! This time, however, we walked through no problems. I even stopped with my bags to talk to a couple of the customs guys, joking with them about how they hadn't searched me for drugs! Don't ask!

Bedouin

It's down another road I go
but I never get home
I looked around to see
watch the darkness grow
there's a box for your mind
a box for your soul
your spirit's inside
never growing old
I keep on trying
but I never get it right
I keep on fighting
try to reach the light

I saw the beast rising from the sand
there he was, just a man
you can't deceive anybody
you can't believe everybody

I saw my brother heading home
saw my father all alone
I know my sister never lied
found my mother when she cried
I saw the beast rising from the sand
the devil's work, just a man
I realised another way
another time, another place
there were times I was blinded
the hidden road, I decided

experiencing a new kind of

blues

By SHANE SUTTON

LUE Experience's aptly titled new EP, *Future Traditions*, is a brand new template, serving as a stylistic beacon for the band's new style.

...the group (pictured at ...bout seven years ago, ...riter, lead guitarist ...member, Simon ...arch to find its ...st come to ...honed, ...ead on the

...the EP is still ...m more tradi... ...yle-base... ...has...

spirit of freedom from spending time on the coast and living under the stars.

Having first started with a more traditional, hard rocking format, Hartley says the addition of a keyboard player less than a year ago has significantly changed the group, as has the addition of backing vocalist Kylena Vigus.

"We had a guitar-based hard rock sound, although st... nal in its earlier stag... addition of keyboards ... do a lot of things th... wanting to try ...

...which ... although ... ...yle-base... has...

experiences ha... free from styl...

Before w... more like mo... viously rock o... says. "But the ...and it is no l... that the mus...

"The ...

Chapter Eleven

BERLIN AND THE ZOMBIE HOMING PIGEON

Sometimes the truth ain't so great, not when the illusion is more beautiful

It was the first time Kylea and I had a house to ourselves, and we were doing okay. We didn't have a lot of money, or much of an income, but we loved each other, we had a group of friends, a pretty good lifestyle, and a bit of time. If Kylea was happy, I was okay. Well, apart from the truckload of drugs I was using; and I was still hiding my heroin addiction. We went on a few trips up the east coast. I was used to the long hauls and could drive twenty-four hours straight. Leaving the Adelaide Hills, we would drive across the Hay Plains, past the mountains of country NSW, and straight on to the east coast of northern NSW and Queensland. I was still surfing, and we camped in some remote and beautiful places overlooking the Pacific Ocean.

Triple J Radio reaches more people than any other radio station in Australia. If you got airplay on Triple J, you had national attention, and with that, at least a glimmer of hope. My dream, dare I say it, was to make a living writing, playing, and recording music. You can guess what happened to that dream. Forget about dreams, look for opportunities!

I took a phone call out of the blue, and it was Triple J in Sydney. They asked me if the band would play live in the ABC studios. That was a great experience, and we had a good session, although we were put under a lot of pressure when there were sound problems, a lack of time and almost no sound check. Kylena had natural talent but she was still a young and inexperienced vocalist, and sometimes suffered from a lack of confidence. She cracked under the pressure and the producer removed her vocals. Despite that disappointment, we had a good sound and we played well enough. We certainly had an original style, especially with Taz on keys. We had some fat, swampy organ sounds, gritty guitars and funky beats. The producer liked it and Triple J played it nationally, with a couple of songs put on rotation, several times a day.

EMI rang. It was one of the executives. He had heard our live performance and was excited about the song, *I Can See It Coming*. The problem was the song he liked had a very particular organ sound. Taz had kind of stumbled on that sound in the studio at the last minute to replace Kylena's vocals. The EMI exec asked me if I could send him more songs with that sound, and although we didn't have any, I said, "Yeah, of course, no worries." At the time, Taz was studying hard and about to hit some major exams, and we had just finished a tour of the east coast. We did not have the time or finances to go back into a recording studio.

I sent EMI a few songs which had a bit more of a rocky edge to them and not the organ sound he was after. To his credit, Mr Record Company Executive did call back to say that they liked the songs, but they were a little too "retro." He was right. Blue Experience was retro. I'm sure you will agree that it was the '60s and '70s that produced many of the all-time great bands.

It was time for another big change, but what? I pressured the band for more commitment. I got the opposite, and the band reached the end. My timing has never been good, and I had always asked a lot - too much, in fact. It wasn't as if anyone was getting paid much, if anything; and maybe the band had just run its course. It was 1997 and it had been ten years, gigging every week. I had supported bands like Chain, The Tea Party and Powderfinger, played festivals and toured the country, enjoying quite a bit of airplay, including live on Triple J. Sometimes life can change dramatically and abruptly. The road I was heading down was always going to be a slow train coming, and the train had no brakes! As my drug use increased, so did my lack of inspiration and motivation. Any flair with music I may have had disappeared. I tried jamming with some different musicians, but I was terrible. I was a drug addict. I felt like a shell of my former self, and I quit music in despair.

We were broke, so instead of going out and getting a job like most people do, I set up two large rooms in the house with an elaborate hydroponic system. I installed high voltage growing lights, ventilation and irrigation equipment, and installed extraction fans in each room. I had an electrician bypass all the safety switches in the meter box on the house because we were drawing so much current the safety switches kept tripping. It was running 24/7.

I had two rooms in different growth stages, with as many plants as possible, and a separate area for growing cuttings. It's amazing how hot it gets in those rooms even with multiple fans. In fact, you can get sunburnt in a couple of minutes. Everything was set on timers, so most of the work that needed doing could be done when the lights were off. It was easy enough to get the hang of it and we were harvesting every twelve weeks. With regard to State law, the risk became much higher when it was time to harvest. If the plants were in pots and you had ten plants or less, you would incur a hefty fine and have your equipment confiscated. If the plants were harvested, you would be charged with possession with intent to sell, and that would mean a date in court and possible jail time. As you can imagine, harvesting was a little stressful.

After about a year, we booked a three-week holiday in England and Germany. This was my first time back in England for about seventeen years or so, and Kylea was as excited as

I was. We started in London, which is a tad different from Aldinga. We arrived at about 4am and immediately went for a walk through the back streets. We got stopped by a hip, local black guy in his early twenties asking for money. He offered to show us around for a few quid.

It soon became apparent that he wasn't going to be much of a guide, though. I pointed to Nelson's Column and said, "Who's that?"

He replied without hesitation and very confidently, "That, my friend, is some French geezer!"

Kylea loved London and after just a day or two said, "I feel like I have come home." I thought that was strange, but I liked it.

We hired a car and headed off to Manchester and The Lakes District. We spent a night at the famous Haçienda night club in Manchester, about ten years too late. We both got way too drunk, and the bouncers threw me out - literally! Kylea emerged about an hour later with a group of locals, looking as if she had lived there all her life. We had a terrible fight fuelled by alcohol and to make things worse, I drove back to the hotel like a bloody madman in the ridiculously fast sports car we'd hired. The next morning, we headed back to London, before heading out to Berlin.

The night before we left, Kylea went shopping all day and I walked into a hairdresser and asked them to cut off my ten-year-old dreadlocks and, while they were at it, to dye whatever hair was left jet black. It took four hours and I fell asleep. When they woke me, I did a jump scare on myself. I was looking at my reflection but seeing someone else. We went out to dinner that night a bit more dressed up than usual, and with me sporting a brand-new look. The friendly taxi driver asked me what I did for a living, and I lied and said I was a musician. Sometimes the truth ain't so great, not when the illusion is more beautiful. He dropped us at a very high-end restaurant called The Ivy. With a different haircut, a little money, and some new clothes, we found that people treated us differently. We were in another world - temporarily!

The next morning, we arrived in Berlin and booked into a 5-star hotel in the middle of the city. We immediately headed for East Berlin in a boat on the River Spree. It appeared grim as we passed gypsy camps, abandoned factories and run-down empty buildings. That night, Kylea stayed in our room as she was recovering from food poisoning, ironically picked up from the most expensive and exclusive restaurant we had ever eaten in. I went down to the sophisticated and trendy bar in the hotel and slowly drank two Bloody Marys. The barman seemed amicable and interesting, and we chatted about the underground music scene in Berlin. The barman was probably in his early thirties, and we seemed to make a connection, or so I thought. He offered to show me around, as he was about to knock off for the night. I came back from the toilet and saw a full shot glass on the bar.

"Hey, man, it's on the house – a local specialty."

Yeah, a local specialty all right. The bastard had spiked it! It was fortunate that I had built up a serious tolerance to drugs and alcohol over the years because boy, was it powerful, like nothing I ever experienced, and I thought I had done it all. As soon as I put the glass down, he called a taxi and we left. After a few minutes, I knew I was in trouble. I can only recall bits and pieces, but I remember the first thing I did. I took all my money, about 300 Euros, out of my wallet. I knew I was going to get robbed and I didn't want to give them my wallet.

It was a strange experience and difficult to explain, but whatever the drug was, I couldn't speak, and it made me passive and compliant. It was strange. I knew he had drugged me, and yet I went along with whatever he said. Fortunately, he was just after money. It was as though I was under hypnosis. I was trying desperately hard to fight it, focus, and not pass out. I sat in the taxi and watched as we drove miles into East Berlin. The next thing I remember, I was staggering down some stairs into a club and seeing my new best friend talking to a very unpleasant-looking woman and disappearing through a back door. I said *a* back door, not *her* back door!

I have tried to recall all the events of that night, but there are some big gaps. I know I gave that woman all my money, as she was twisting my balls so hard, I thought they were going to pop. Something hit me in the side of the head, and I found myself outside the club, lying in the street, covered in blood, bruises and vomit. I had absolutely no idea where I was or how I would get back to the hotel. I had only been in the country a few hours, I had no money, and I was so fucked up I couldn't talk, let alone speak German. I had lost the ability to even think straight, I could hardly walk, and when I did walk, I looked like a zombie! Fortunately, I'd had so much experience fucking myself up on drugs and alcohol, I think it ironically saved my life.

Whatever it was the barman had slipped into my drink, it was way too much. I dragged myself up and started walking, or to be more specific, staggering. I don't know how I did it, but I went from scary-weird-zombie-man into weird-zombie-homing-pigeon-man. Somehow, about eight to ten hours later, I made it back to the hotel, without even looking up! Anyone I came across on the street I let know - and not too subtly - that I held them responsible. To my complete and utter shame, I have a sneaky suspicion that I may have thrown in a few *Heil Hitlers* along the way. When I got back to the hotel, I still had the challenge of finding my room. I needed help but there seemed to be a lack of volunteers. I found myself doing many trips in the elevator and snarling at whoever was there when the doors opened. Eventually, a housemaid helped me to my room, but not before I had smashed as many vases, paintings, and ornaments as I could get my hands on. I staggered into the room, saw the horrified look on Kylea's face, and passed out.

When I came around, I tried to explain what had happened as she had been up half the night worrying about my disappearance. As I talked through the night's events, I started to recall more and more details. I had crawled, walked, staggered and fallen, over and over, all night; but I still have no idea how I found my way back. I hadn't bothered to remember the name of the hotel we were staying in or the street it was on, as Kylea had made all the bookings.

I had mixed pills with alcohol for years, including very powerful drugs like Rohypnol, but I have never experienced anything like that. It was the acquiescence that puzzled me. For the next couple of days, I was incredibly sick, and everything turned green, inside, and out. I tried to complain at reception, but as soon as I arrived at the front desk, I was surrounded by staff accusing me of being drunk and damaging property. When I attempted to explain that I'd had just two drinks, they didn't want to know about it and their English seemed to deteriorate, until we couldn't even have a conversation, let alone an argument. Of course, the barman was conveniently away for a few days.

We left early, caught a plane to London and flew back home.

Mad and Bad

I'm going to find my way home
This is it, as far as I go
There's a reason that I know
It is time to let it all go
I can see right through the trees
Now I know what it means
Why it's taken all these years
Just to realise my fears

Like a ship that's out to sea
I can sail into the breeze
Let the waves roll underneath
Don't care how dark and deep
There's a void now in my brain
Nothing here stays the same
All I've given, all I've lost
I don't care about the cost

No-one here escapes their fate
Pulled from dark
The line goes straight
I'm mad and bad
Wild at heart
Carry my cross
Follow that star

I can stay here by your side
Love you now for all my life
All I do is let you go
There's nothing else I need to know.

Chapter Twelve

BUSTED

You're a long time dead

A hydroponic system needs liquid nutrients, which we bought from a small warehouse in an industrial estate at Lonsdale. It was run by some young guys who were really into it and obviously growing their own crops. The problem was, the cops had put them under surveillance, and they casually pointed the police out to me AFTER I had loaded the car up with supplies.

"Shiii-eeeet," I said, in my best Mississippi Delta accent, "now you tell me! I bet that's good for business."

"Don't worry about it, man, there's not much they can do." He gave them the finger and walked into the warehouse, leaving me standing there like a sitting duck, or a standing duck.

"Great," I said out loud, to no-one. "Nothing they can do. Only take down my number plate, get my address, and pop round the house."

Sure enough, within a few days, I started to notice the cops taking an interest, driving slowly past the house. There wasn't much I could do, other than quit altogether or reduce the size of the crop. I moved the whole operation into a local day care centre,(Joking, obviously! It wasn't a day care centre; it was a kindergarten. No, I moved the drying process to another property and reduced the number of plants.

One night, all the power went out. I had bypassed the safety switches in the meter box and gone straight from the street to the house. I had blown the fuse in the pole down the street and seeing as all the neighbours were standing in the street looking at the pole, I presumed their power had gone out too. The crew arrived the next morning to do repairs, and a few days later, I came home from the shops with Kylea to find four police cars and a van in the driveway. I wasn't sure what to do, so I kept driving.

One of the community-minded neighbours very kindly pointed me out to the police as I drove past, and they jumped into one of the patrol cars, ready for a high-speed pursuit. I was doing about twenty when they caught up with us. We had just enough time to hide a large wad of cash and tickets to Europe. I pulled over and got out of the car. The cop was angry and started yelling at me and got all animated. I drove back to the house. They were inside and smashing the lights and equipment. There were police all through the house, but they didn't find the heroin and they didn't think to look in the car.

They were pissed off and frustrated because I had just under the amount for prosecution in court, and I was sticking to my ridiculous story of personal use. I had moved a substantial amount just a few days earlier, and they found nothing dried and packaged. They made me stand outside in front of my neighbours, and by that, I mean the whole fucking street. There were so many people hanging around, I started to look for food trucks and an ice cream van. It must have been very entertaining. The police finished up and left me with a large fine and a real mess. We spent the next week fixing the house, painting, and moving out. We flew out to Europe a few days later. We went to Italy and the UK but ran out of money quickly. We talked about staying, but I was really struggling with my addiction, and the heroin and methadone I had smuggled with me all over Europe had run out.

We headed back to Australia and moved into a caravan park by the beach. It was an idyllic few weeks in autumn with perfect weather, and we were falling asleep to the sound of waves breaking on the beach. After a month or so, I went cold turkey and managed to get clean. I just started to feel better, when late one night, an old friend found us and talked me into taking a hit with him. It was the old cliché: "Come on man, just a one-off, for old times' sake." A few weeks later that friend became involved with a real criminal and got caught up in an armed robbery. The car he used as the getaway vehicle had a broken clutch and was stuck in second gear. The business owner, who had just been robbed at gun point, had no problem following them home at a top speed of about thirty. The other guy was gunned down by police, and my friend went to jail.

After a desperate time of getting clean, I was back to square one. That's how it works. It's a disease. I was sick. And when someone offers you a cure or relief, no matter how temporary, it becomes very hard to say no. The next morning, I was dealing with the horror of withdrawals, dread, and desperation. I went to the altar, and the Devil welcomed me back with open arms!

Kylea was adamant we look for a legitimate and honest way to make a living. We found an old run-down shop in a local seaside town with a small house attached to it. We moved in and started renovating. We worked tirelessly for months and turned it into a Southeast Asian takeaway. Kylea has an eye for design, colour and detail, and it looked great. I ran the kitchen and Kylea ran the front of house. We hired a few staff and started our first legitimate business.

The problem was my heroin addiction had become full blown. Life was extremely difficult. I was getting by one day at a time as best I could, and without letting Kylea down. I was seriously sick and trapped in a nightmare. There comes a time when all you do is try to function and avoid the sickness, there is no high. What could I do? I loved Kylea, yet I was keeping a hideous secret from her. I had become a full-blown junkie. Kylea found out soon enough anyway, when she walked in on me shooting up in the bathroom, and the shit hit the fan. I went up to the Hills to confess to my poor old mum and made an appointment to see a doctor.

The doctor was a specialist who lived and worked in the city. He was allowed to prescribe restricted painkillers and opiate-based drugs. I was prescribed methadone, a powerful, nasty, and highly addictive substitute for heroin. Developed by the Nazis in 1937, it was supposed to help by getting you off the streets. It is heavily regulated, cheap, and administered daily from a chemist in carefully measured doses. Of course, they don't warn you about the side-effects, which include your teeth falling out, severe constipation, stomach cramps, sweating, and the anxious highs and terrible lows; not to mention the withdrawals you get in the early mornings while you wait, every day, for the chemist to open. What had I done to myself?

I had stopped surfing the cool, pristine waters of the Great Southern Ocean, where I had made a deep connection with nature. I had also given up on my ability to write, play and record music, and for what? To become a sad and desperate junkie! The biggest mistake of my life was trying heroin. My second biggest mistake was not getting a second opinion and finding an excellent and caring doctor, My third biggest mistake was taking methadone. I had a business to run and a woman to love.

We opened the restaurant six days a week and in our first year won a small business award for best restaurant. We worked long hours for two and a half years, until we were offered a good price for the business. Job done. I will share one story with you from that time. We had just opened, when a young and inebriated dickhead decided to go around the neighbourhood, kicking in shop windows. We lived out the back and were in bed when we heard what sounded like a bomb going off, as next door's plate glass window exploded. It sounded as if someone had driven a truck through the place. I leapt out of bed, caught Kylea's knee, and face planted. My adrenaline was pumping so I jumped up and ran into the restaurant, flicking the lights on.

Everything moved in slow motion as several things happened at the same time. This bloke stuck his boot through our window, the lights came on, and I realised I had no clothes on. The window flew all around me, spraying the place in glass fragments. I saw the shocked look on his face as the lights came on and he saw me standing in the middle of the restaurant, naked. I heard him say, "Geez, that's a big one." Okay, that's not true; he just legged it. I took off after him and I didn't have time to put any clothes on. Lucky for me, he had practically cut his foot in half, so he was more hobbling than running, and the police were in the area. He got arrested for criminal damage. I was arrested for tea bagging!

Damn shame that last bit ain't true. It would have made a great headline in the morning paper.

A couple of months later, we were cruising down the NSW southern coast. I had a prescribed supply of methadone in pill form, rather than the daily dose you had to drink in front of the chemist. I was taking 10mg tablets, ten times a day. God knows why, as that was an unnecessary and ridiculously high dose. One-tenth of that could kill the average human. We stayed in a small town called Milton, next to a beautiful surf beach. We heard that Stuart Wilde lived in the area during the summer months. Stuart was a famous, wealthy, and successful self-help author and public speaker. Or, as he liked to put it, "the Drinking Man's Guru". He had some cool knowledge, ideas, and a practical philosophy. Unfortunately, we soon discovered that Stuart was also a little too fond of alcohol, drugs, cigarettes, money, and women.

Kylea and I had listened to a lot of his seminars and audio tapes and read most of his books and they had struck a chord with both of us. We found his work intriguing, and he was a bit of an enigma. It's strange how things work out. Our first day in town, we went to a local store and struck up a conversation with the owner. She mentioned she knew Stuart and that he was looking to hire someone to cook and clean for him and his eight-year-old son.

We drove up to his place in the mountains, overlooking a temperate rain forest. It was a stunning location. Stuart had hired a very talented builder to design and build a mansion that would have looked more at home in Morocco. It had a roof-top swimming pool and nearly thirty rooms on three levels, including hidden passages, special rooms with secret doors, and a dragon in a cave. Well, okay, there was no cave, and the dragon was a squeaky toy, but the house was amaze balls! We were hired on the spot with generous pay, food, and our own room. Our job was to cook all the meals, shop, look after guests and help with the care of his son Sebastian. Stuart had been through a recent and difficult divorce. I think the main reason we were hired and offered free accommodation, however, was that perhaps Stuart had been a bit bedazzled by the young and gorgeous Kylea. It was November 1999.

We had a week to get back to Adelaide, move out of the flat we rented, sell most of our belongings and drive back to Milton a thousand miles away. As soon as we were back in Adelaide, I went to my doctor and asked him for his help getting off the methadone.

"Sure, Simon, it's not that difficult. I can get you a bed in the local hospital for a night. I will arrange it for you straight away."

"Really? How does that work?"

"Don't worry about it, Simon. It's all in your head. It will just be a little uncomfortable."

I was desperately keen to get off the methadone, but I was really surprised, even shocked by the doctor's reaction. If it was that easy, why hadn't he mentioned it before, and why was I on such a high dose?

"No problems," he said. "Let me organise it.'"

I was admitted into hospital a couple of days later and met the nurse in charge, who didn't seem to know what was going on. My doctor didn't show up. Another nurse who had just started her shift came in to speak with me; it was very brief, and she only had the barest of information. It seemed no-one there had any expertise in dealing with a drug detox. In that hospital I was the first, and as it would turn out, the last.

I became concerned and started having second thoughts. I knew that coming off a massive dose of methadone could potentially be fatal. I decided I had reached the point of no return, and I was, after all, in a hospital! I said goodbye to Kylea, went to my room and waited for my descent into hell. I was on an extremely high dose, probably enough to kill a fucking hippo! I would hazard a guess that it was roughly eight times my previous heroin use. I went into shock a few hours later when the receptors in my brain registered that the massive supply of opiates had stopped, just like that. No counselling, no medication, no reduction, nothing. I should have been given a week in a padded cell. I got through the normal side-effects of vomiting, stomach cramps, diarrhoea, anxiety, sweating and shaking, but this was on another level, and I moved on to the next stage. I started tearing at my skin, hallucinating, and convulsing. I turned into a depraved lunatic; I would have stopped at nothing for it to end!

It's hard to explain the sheer terror that encapsulates you. It's as though you have been buried alive. It was almost impossible to breathe, and I thought I was going to die. I bashed my head against the wall, attempting to knock myself out. My vision went, and I was shaking so much I couldn't even stand. I was screaming for help when the nurse came in and I pleaded for her to give me something, anything. I was rolling around on the floor, banging my head on the ground and tearing at my skin, when she gave me a dose of methadone. I woke up about twelve hours later and was discharged without seeing a doctor.

That little experiment my doctor put me through was never repeated at that hospital. The nurses who were on duty that night put in a complaint, and I'm glad they did. I would not wish that kind of suffering on anyone! I saw my doctor at his private clinic in the city the next day.

"So that went well, Simon," he said, with a chuckle. "The nurse rang me at three in the morning and said you were having trouble. I prescribed you three of the 10mg tablets."

Of course, it was my fault!

"I think you panicked a bit there, Simon. You could have gotten through it. It's all in your head; it's psychological, you see,"

"No, that's not right. I nearly died. I couldn't breathe."

He just laughed. "Look, the good news is you have dropped your dose from 100 milligrams to thirty, so well done. I'll write you a script for a few months and you can go away for work. When you get back, we can try again. Perhaps we could try some hypnotherapy."

That's when I pulled out the gun and shot him between the eyes. He fell to the floor, and I unloaded the chamber into his lifeless corpse! I sat down in his chair and relaxed, put my feet on his desk, adjusted my hat and enjoyed a cigarette while

I waited for the police to arrive. I remember thinking, *Geez, I really should quit smoking*.

Hang on, dreaming again.

I was still trapped, and my doctor was my drug dealer, that's how I saw it. I was seriously addicted to methadone, which was strictly regulated. I had to play nice and put up with his callous, arrogant behaviour!

I got my prescription and we set off on another road trip across inland Australia. We were heading for the coastal town of Milton once more. All we had with us was our cat Treacle, and some clothes. We moved into Stuart's mansion and, to begin with, it was interesting and enjoyable. The work was not particularly difficult and although the house was huge, most rooms were unused. There was a steady stream of young visitors, mainly from the US and Europe. Some would stay a few days, some a few weeks. I had a supply of methadone, which I took every day. I tried to ignore the side-effects and get on with it as best as I could, and I did a good job of hiding it.

New Year's Eve 1999 sneaked up on us, and about twenty or so people in their early and late thirties seemed to arrive out of nowhere. That night, everyone got high, and Stuart offered us some MDMA (ecstasy). We took half of what was offered – a quarter of what everyone else had. We disappeared from the party early to be together in a beautiful Japanese-themed room, with dozens of razor-sharp Samurai swords hanging on the walls.

We spent six months working for Stuart through a long hot summer, and it was an interesting experience. You can learn a lot from a dysfunctional charlatan, and you can extract value from things you don't like! We did try to help Stuart. He was still suffering from his divorce and was deteriorating, physically and mentally. I imagine that in his better days, Stuart could have been charismatic and charming, just like my father; but Stuart was on a downhill run by the time we met him, and his divorce was the catalyst for a full meltdown. He was drinking heavily, smoking up to three packets of cigarettes a day, he ate terribly, and he was taking medication to sleep. He claimed to be a wizard.

Just before we walked out, Stuart had about twenty guests arrive, mainly couples. There was to be a week-long workshop and retreat. They had paid $5000 each and Stuart had done no preparation and was having trouble holding it together. He thought of himself as a guru but had about as much to teach his guests as the town drunk. It was sad to see, but Stuart was ripping everyone off.

He was showing off one evening when he hit one of the guests in the head with a sword, cutting him badly. Another guest had his ribs broken when Stuart punched him. Apparently, it was supposed to be a gentle push so the guest could pass into another dimension! The guest did not reach another dimension, but he did reach a hospital. Stuart also had sex with one of the women, who was at the workshop with her husband. Two couples broke up, leading to a lot of tears and arguing. There was some heavy drinking at night, which left everyone feeling hungover and sick the next day, and the house got trashed. All very spiritual, I know.

It was so bad we grabbed our gear and left. We found a beautiful house on the beach. It was the ideal hideaway, tucked into a little forest, on a headland. It was late summer, and we enjoyed a taste of paradise for a month or so, walking down the garden and into the Pacific Ocean.

It is one of my fondest memories. We were on our own, and we were happy. It was hard to leave, but my supply of methadone was running low, and I needed to see my doctor, or preferably get a referral to see another doctor, one who could help.

I'll sail against the wind

and ride the darkest seas

Fly above the desert dunes

The night fall Comes to me

I climb towards the highest ledge

Feels like falling

Alone in bed

Dreams are fading

Hear her breath

All i fear

All is red

I'm waking now

In broken chains

Invisible i find

Feel the pain

The silence I fear

Hear her roar

The night time circus

On my wall

I open up

Walk right in

Ancestors call

Shed my skin

Feed the courage

A fire inside

Within my heart

Within my eye

-SH

Chapter Thirteen

DESOLATION

**The flame will burn brighter indeed the
more you look inside and see**

We were back in Adelaide and living in a flat close to the city centre. Kylea got a job across the road at a fancy café, and I went to see my doctor about getting off methadone. He suggested switching from methadone to a new drug called Subutex which contains Buprenorphine, another opiate-based product. What I didn't know at the time was that Subutex was primarily designed to wean people off heroin and/or methadone and is prescribed for short-term use of six weeks or less.

I have been told by two psychiatrists, a researcher from Flinders University, a nurse from DASA, and a GP, that they are not aware of anyone in Australia being subscribed Subutex for as long as I was. Subutex was designed to aid in the withdrawal process. I was prescribed Subutex for nineteen years. My doctor consistently told me to accept that I was a lifer. No research has been done on the long-term use of Subutex and no research has been done on what happens when someone stops! This begs the question: Why? Why was I prescribed Subutex for nineteen years? Well, I will get to that later! Great question though, thanks for asking.

Switching from one shit drug to another shit drug is not easy. I became extremely ill and occasionally would look for an easier way out. It's a slippery slope and I was nearing the bottom. I tried other doctors, but they refused to help, mainly because they didn't know me and thought I was doctor shopping. Sometimes they would ring my doctor, and he did not like that. On a couple of occasions, he rang me and angrily demanded that I not talk to anyone about my treatment. I went back to him again, as I was still trying to get clean. This time, he suggested Naltrexone. Naltrexone suppresses cravings for opiates by binding to the opiate receptors in the brain. It is an opiate antagonist; if you use heroin while on Naltrexone, you will not get high. One of the problems, however, is that you can only take Naltrexone after you have completely stopped using opiates for a minimum of five days. In other words, Naltrexone is used to prevent former addicts from re-using. It is for prevention. The critical thing here is whatever happens, do not to take Naltrexone if you have any - and I mean any - opiates in your system. Uh-oh!

My doctor had rung Kylea and asked her to make sure I took the naltrexone every day. Kylea confronted me one night with a dose and became upset with me when I tried to talk my way out of taking it. I eventually agreed, but just pretended to swallow the pill and hid it under my tongue. What Kylea didn't know was that a few hours earlier, I had injected a huge dose of high-grade heroin. I tried to remove the tablet, but it had dissolved! I had no idea what was coming. If I had, I would have called an ambulance.

I sat down and waited. Half an hour later, I was in the worst condition of my life. I tried to use the phone to call for help but I couldn't see the keypad and my hands were shaking terribly. I thought dying would be a better option. I found some rope and attempted to tie a noose. I couldn't even do that. I tried to get Professor Plum in the library with the candlestick to do the deed, but no. I started to experience sharp stabbing pains in my brain and zaps like electric shocks, as the Naltrexone tore the opiates from the receptors in my brain. It was excruciatingly painful, like nothing I had ever experienced. It made coming down off methadone look like a picnic.

The shocks to the brain increased and I started crying out in agony and rolling around the floor. It was the most horrific experience. At one point I felt a powerful band expand around my chest. It was sitting a few inches off my chest, and it encompassed my whole being. It's impossibly hard to describe, but it was suffocating, and I couldn't breathe. I thought I was going to die, again!

I was fighting for my life for four hours until I passed out. I had of course woken Kylea up and completely freaked her out. She had rung my doctor, but when Kylea suggested ringing an ambulance, he said, "No, leave him alone and he will eventually be okay." It was a bloody miracle I didn't choke to death, have a heart attack, stroke, or aneurysm, let alone die by hanging. I had just survived a week-long detox in about four hours.

I went back to my doctor again and got the usual comments, such as, "Well, at least you're still alive." I was as sick as one could get, and worse than that, I could not sleep. I also developed a terrible and frightening condition called akathisia! This is an uncontrollable urge to move, shake, tremble, and twitch.Sounds like a new dance craze, but it does not stop and it's exhausting, physically and mentally.

I needed time to rehabilitate. I had to take responsibility for my choices and change my behaviour. It sounds so bloody obvious and straightforward, but believe me, drug addiction is a disease that changes the way you think, feel, and behave. It changes your brain chemistry, and it changes you. At the time I could not accept or even see what I had become. However, I tried, and about five weeks later, I was still clean. I was not in good health, mainly because I could not sleep. On a good night, I'd fall asleep for a few minutes around sunrise. I tried all sorts of sleeping tablets and took them like smarties, but the more I took, the worse I got. I swallowed a whole packet one night and, paradoxically, it was like amphetamines - not recommended!

While I was struggling through this, Dad rang out of the blue and invited me to join him and my younger brother Ben on another dive trip, this time to PNG. I took no drugs with me this time, apart from four packets of sleeping tablets for a ten-day trip. We caught a couple of very dodgy light planes, island hopping until we arrived in the very north of PNG. The boat was a one-hundred-foot-long, three-deck catamaran, designed for cruising the shallow waters around the islands of the Pacific Ocean. It had a crew of twelve and around fifteen divers. I dived every day, three or four times a day, and it really started to help my recovery. It was an adventure, and we dived on Second World War shipwrecks, planes, and even a Japanese mini submarine. We also dived with sharks, including a large group (shiver) of hammerheads, and we dived at night.

I got my diving licence as a seventeen-year-old at Palm Beach near Sydney and seeing as I seemed so confident while training in the pool, the instructor decided to take me straight to the ocean and down one hundred and fifty feet on my first dive! It was just the two of us, in a little dinghy a mile out to sea and 150 feet down. What a plonker! We checked our gear, and without saying much, we hit the water and headed down. I followed the instructor as he descended into the darkness. We came to the ocean floor, at which point he swam off towards a shipwrecked ferry. I lost sight of him for a while but spotted him on the deck waving to the fish and acting as though he was on a cruise across the bloody harbour. It was bizarre, and it was my first dive! I learned after the dive that recreational divers never go that deep; there's very little light, no colour, and it's dangerous. The main reason, however, is the risk of nitrogen narcosis, which is akin to being high or drunk. It can be very dangerous, and every diver has heard stories of someone at the bottom of the ocean losing their minds, taking off their equipment and disappearing into the deep blue.

Towards the end of the dive trip, Ben and I took an advanced diving course. The last part of that was a written exam, made up of chemistry and maths equations, not exactly my area of expertise. I had a not-so-subtle plan and waited for Ben, who is very smart, to finish his paper. I copied Ben's paper exactly. Well, almost. It looked suspect, so Ben went over my answers in the multiple-choice sections and changed a few answers, just enough to not get caught. About an hour later, my cabin door burst open. Ben was standing there, looking slightly pissed off. Somehow, I had scored higher, and to make it even more sweet, the instructor gave Ben a little telling off.

"Dear me, Ben, you should take note of how well your brother's done. He's got an almost perfect score!"

I killed myself laughing! The look on his face was priceless.

The next dive, Ben and I left a small group of divers and headed out to the open ocean. We followed a ledge towards a huge drop, and I headed down, leaving Ben at around eighty feet. I stopped at 160 feet, hoping to get nitrogen narcosis, otherwise known as being narked. My equipment sounded an alarm and flashed warning lights, but I ignored them. It was bliss and I stayed there for a few minutes. After all those sleepless nights, it was euphoria, and I don't think I have ever felt so good. I looked up from the seabed to see Ben bobbing around in the middle of the ocean, frantically waving at me to come back up, I could see his eyes bulging from a hundred feet away. He was too sensible to follow me down. At that depth, I only had a few minutes until I wouldn't have enough air to surface, not without succumbing to the bends. I reluctantly joined Ben and started the slowest ascent I have ever done, decompressing three times, and almost running out of air.

I am convinced that getting narked like that, just for a few minutes, vastly helped in my recovery. Back on deck, I broke my depth gauge so the staff would not see how deep I had gone, then I went straight to my room and threw away the sleeping tablets. That night I got my first proper sleep in a decade. The last night on board, in the middle of the Pacific Ocean, I went around the back of the yacht and found some locals who had paddled out on canoes. We talked for hours in the dark, underneath the most beautiful night sky you will ever see anywhere on Earth. It was like another world. Everything was real, yet at the same time it felt like a dream. It's a hard life for the locals, to live that way in nature, exposed to the elements, but it is also, honest, spectacular, and beautiful.

If you have not witnessed the stars a thousand miles away from all light, you are missing something truly profound, unique, and inspiring. There is such breathtaking depth in the night sky that you feel you can reach up and touch it.

Let the Sun Shine Down on You

Eyes like points of flame
Hear the wind, feel the rain

Giant killer on a wine-dark sea
Let it go so you can be
Black angels
Young men dead
Hopeless lovers covered in red
Dancing with the devil, why?
She speaks the truth
Love is a verb and
They said it was you

Now my fingers on the trigger
All I see is a flame
Heart full of menace
And it's pumping like a train
My soul is like an arrow
I know my arrow's aim
Life is like a river
It'll never be the same
Looking down on a dark night's ocean
A mother's fear and kind devotion
Threads of time, specks of dust
It's just a dream that ends in love

I've worked so hard and paid my dues
Made mistakes and played the blues
I look at it like a cat with nine lives
I'm still here and I survive
Now don't run scared, rest assured
No more bad signs at my door
There's something here for you and I
Are you ready to share the ride?

Let the sun shine down on you.

Chapter Fourteen

SINNERMAN

Perhaps it's not so much about knowing oneself
Rather, creating who it is you want to be

It's hard to rationalise now, but the second day back from the trip, and fully recovered, I relapsed! What was I thinking?

I wasn't thinking. And to be totally honest, I can't explain the choices I made and was still making. It's as though I had subconsciously decided that I needed to suffer. I obviously hadn't recovered at all and needed professional help, particularly in a psychological sense. I hadn't talked about WHY I had an addiction with anyone, let alone a professional. In retrospect, it seems strange that during the time I had away with Dad it was never mentioned. We didn't talk about it, and it didn't occur to me to bring it up. It's a bit sad, really, and as Dad recently passed away, it is now too late.

I will take the blame for that. I missed an opportunity to at least try and bridge a gap that had been there forever. It's not as if we didn't have time. We had been on a boat in the middle of the Pacific Ocean for two weeks, with nothing to do in the day except scuba dive, and at night, sit and marvel at the breathtaking beauty of a star-filled sky. We had no technology, no phones, television, or radio. It was Paradise Found. If we couldn't talk then, when would we? I think we both had the proverbial wall up. Mine was at least partly from Dad walking out on the family, and I imagine Dad had some unresolved issues of his own from the time his mother walked out on his father. I had a dream recently.

I woke up

In the middle of a lake

Standing on an old dead tree

Crocodiles in the water

I thought I could escape and jumped in

My arms were heavy and weak

I pushed one croc

Punched another

Suddenly

My arms felt light and strong

I swam to shore

Looking back

I couldn't see Dad

I shouted

"Dad, Dad, where are you?"

Bottom line, I was back where I started. I overdosed in the car, with the door open, at a local shopping centre. I didn't even have time to get the needle out of my arm before passing out. I came around, sitting in the car covered in vomit and being shaken awake by a good Samaritan. He gave me a bottle of water, which I poured over my head, and then I tried to breathe my way back to the land of the living. I was fighting my way up the tunnel AGAIN, towards the light, away from the dark, just like when I was a kid in the hospital. I wish I could have thanked him. He didn't ring the police and he stayed with me until I managed to communicate that I was okay. He probably saved my life!

I think I overdosed at least fifteen times over the years. It is difficult to understand just how addictive heroin is, mentally and physically. I nearly always used heroin on my own, partly from shame. I did use a few times with friends, junkies, and strangers. In the car one time with an old friend, who is now dead, I opened a packet to prepare a hit, and as soon as we saw the heroin, we started salivating like wild dogs at a kill. My friend vomited. He always did. I could taste that metallic tang with a thought.

Meanwhile, to pay for my habit, I sold most of my musical equipment to pawn shops, including rare, vintage amplifiers, exceptional guitars and boutique, guitar pedals.

I went back to the doctor, the same doctor I had always seen about my addiction. He put me back onto Subutex. As you can imagine, Kylea was getting pretty fed up with the situation and she started to warn me that she would leave if I couldn't get it together. I tried! I found a great location for a new restaurant, and we started to fit out what was an empty space, and it required a huge effort. I worked long hours for months, painting, repairing, and setting up as best I could, with a very limited budget.

One day I entered a chemist and the shop assistant, who had a warm, friendly personality, asked me how she could help. I asked for a syringe, and she asked me what it was for. It took me by surprise, and I suddenly felt embarrassed and ashamed. I was caught off guard. I hesitated and then concocted an unbelievably ridiculous story about injecting glue into a hole in my surfboard that I was repairing. What an idiotic thing to say! She was very helpful and gave me the world's biggest fucking syringe! It was literally for a horse. I got back to the car with just a tiny fragment of dignity left intact, but still desperate to avoid the sickness.

You need to work with what you got, so I prepared the syringe, which, I might add, was almost as big as a pen. I stuck it in my arm, although I was a little apprehensive as there were a lot of people out shopping and walking around the car. It made me nervous, and I drove off with the syringe in my arm. I got as far as the first traffic lights, when a guy on a pushbike pulled up next to me. I had the window down and he looked across. I panicked and pulled the syringe out of my vein. Fuck me! I must have hit an artery. Blood sprayed everywhere, all over the dash and windscreen, and the more I jumped around the car trying to find something to use as a tourniquet, the more it squirted everywhere. It was a blood bath. I have never seen anyone take off on a bicycle so fast - head down, legs pumping and eyes bulging. It was a horror show and he wasn't sticking around for the end. I pulled over, wrapped my arm in a t-shirt and sort of cleaned the blood up with a jumper, luckily without attracting any more attention.

We had a few more setbacks setting up the restaurant than expected, but we finally opened the doors after a few months, and it went off without a hitch. Kylea talked to me again about my drug use and said that I was not the person she had met years before and she wasn't liking the new me. I couldn't see it. It was still me. I was wrong, of course, and I did not heed her warnings.

Kylea had enough and left. I had changed. Everything about me had changed, but I was blinded. Kylea moved into a flat and I found the most horrible place I could find. It was a small, filthy room in a large two-storey mansion in the city. It housed about twenty other sad, lonely, desperate people. I didn't care. I still didn't know how to deal with emotional pain, except perhaps by creating physical pain. I increased my addiction to full-blown junkie status. The single room where I now resided was an indictment of my state of mind. It consisted of a dirty, stained mattress thrown on the floor, one chair, one coffee table, cigarettes, used syringes, spoons and empty heroin packets strewn around the room. Welcome to hell!

I overdosed again and woke up in one of the grimy shower cubicles, with cold water running and no idea how I got there. I crawled to my room, holding back the tears. I was seriously fucked up and ready to die, and it seemed, if I was going to die, I would do it in as shitty a way as possible. I fell asleep. I had a dream, and in the dream, I heard a voice.

Love will always leave a scar

Let it make its mark

For I would not be the same

If not for my broken heart

In my greatest hour of need

I heard an angel's song

I fell asleep and, in my dream,

My love grew ever strong

The next morning, I bought flowers for Kylea, but when I arrived at her flat, she wasn't home. I noticed a window open and climbed in. Not the best idea I've ever had. I climbed through, but as I stood up, I saw a Muslim woman in a hijab cowering in the corner of the room looking terrified.

"Shit, wrong flat!" I quickly blurted out. "Hi, I, err, I'm sorry, I'm in the wrong flat." I gave her a big stupid grin and offered her the flowers as a peace offering. I can imagine that I didn't sound too convincing.

"It's okay, I'll see myself out."

I climbed back out the window, found Kylea's flat next door, and left the flowers on the doorstep.

I joined the best fitness centre in Adelaide and moved out of the cesspit. I went to stay at Dad's place, and I shared a room with my brother Ben. I went to the gym six days a week and used what I had learnt as a kid when I was training with Karl. I went as hard as I could, for at least two hours a day. I wasn't drinking alcohol and I stopped using all drugs except the prescribed Subutex. I changed my diet, and most importantly, my attitude. I went to my doctor every twelve weeks to renew the script, and he rang my family and insisted that I take Naltrexone as it would, he said, prevent me from using. He said it would be okay to take the Naltrexone while taking Subutex.

He was wrong! I had already endured one near-death experience with Naltrexone and within half an hour of taking it again, I was going through the same horror. What would normally be a week-long withdrawal from the opiates was suddenly down to a terrifying and nightmarish four- hour seizure. Of course, when I came around, no-one believed me. I swore that I hadn't used any drugs, because I hadn't, it was the Subutex that had reacted to the Naltrexone. No-one believed me. No-one does when you're a drug addict. Why would they? I had run out of credit years ago. That was the second time I had taken Naltrexone, and it was the last time. Both times nearly killed me.

After a few months, Kylea could see I had changed, and I started to visit her more frequently. I was hoping to start

The Devil Thumbs A Ride

the courting process again. I will never forget the feeling I had on one visit when she turned to me, and we embraced for the first time since breaking up. It was like falling in love again. We stayed together that night, and before long we were looking for a place together.

I had changed my perception to gratitude, and was determined to never, ever, take another step backwards. Within months, Kylea was pregnant with our first daughter, Grace.

Keep on pushing

Walking through the dark

Listen to the silence

Following your heart

Looking with your eyes closed

The sounding of the sea

Hearing gentle music

Falling from the trees

Feeling without touching

Losing never lost

Loving without taking

Understand the cost

Bold as a mountain

Lover's hidden key

Mother's soft embrace

Father set me free

Chapter Fifteen

LOVE AND OTHER DRUGS

Your awareness is a ride to eternity

We found a house to rent and opened another restaurant. We got married, I persisted with the gym six days a week, and I stuck to the medication treatment. The wedding was small and low-key, but Kylea looked stunning and elegant, with a small belly bump where Grace was growing, and I loved her. We had a short holiday, just the two of us on a yacht, sailing around Lake Alexandrina. Grace was born healthy, but it was a challenging and difficult birth, with a thirty-hour labour. I think Kylea found it a bit difficult too! We were entering new waters.

I was seriously busy now, running two restaurants and looking after Grace. I was hands-on with baths, nappies, bedtimes, play and walks, all of which I wouldn't swap for anything in the world. It was, however, becoming increasingly difficult to work long hours and care for a young family.

Subutex is an opiate with many side-effects, the least of which leaves you tired and drowsy. Paradoxically, it can also make you feel very anxious and on edge, as though you have taken amphetamines. I found out many years later that the long-term use of Subutex was giving me severe osteoporosis, liver damage and joint pain. It is a painkiller, but after prolonged use it had paradoxically started to be the cause of constant pain, and I mean constant. The medical profession has no idea what other damage Subutex could do long-term, because there has been no research done in that area, and there never will be. It was never designed to be used long-term. There is no potential to make money by getting people off medication. Who would fund that research?

My time, however, was now! We were living and working in the city and my doctor had told me on more than one occasion that there was only a handful of doctors in SA that could prescribe Subutex, a controlled and regulated drug. I took him at his word and stayed with him. I explained my change in circumstances to him and asked for help in getting off all medication permanently. It wasn't well received. It was, in his opinion, a bad idea. He wrote me another script, insisting that for the time being I should stay the course. Because my attitude and circumstances had changed, I felt ready to turn everything around, and it was a real blow to my confidence when he said, "NO!" I was a husband and a father now and I was absolutely committed to a very different life. It did not feel right that my doctor could refuse my request to get off a highly addictive and damaging medication. It was a setback, but I was determined to prove that I was done taking drugs of any kind.

I took a day off work to meet my mum and sister one warm summer's night. We were going to the outdoor cinema in the parklands, and I offered to park Mum's car for her. I drove a couple of minutes up the road, parked and headed back. Just before I walked in the gates, I turned around to take notice of where I had parked and saw two guys in their early twenties dressed like gangsters in an American hip hop film clip. You know, hoodies, oversized baggy jeans and caps on backwards. I watched them break into Mum's car.

It took a few seconds to register. I was thinking to myself, *Oh, that's weird, that looks exactly like Mum's car. Bloody hell, that is Mum's car.* My first reaction was to yell out, but I stopped myself, remembering that I had done that before on one occasion when I caught some kids stealing Mum's purse, and all that did was give them a head start and it took me about half an hour running through the city to catch them. This time, I kept quiet and casually started jogging over, trying not to look. I got about fifty yards away before they noticed me and jumped out of Mum's car. I sprinted for the one on the driver's side, but he took off, and he was fast. I made a lunge for him as I got close but skidded on the gravel and fell. By the time I got up, I couldn't see him. I stepped into the middle of the road and put my hand up to the first car that came along. The car stopped.

They were a young couple and I jumped in the back and yelled, "GO!" They looked completely freaked out and didn't say a word as we sped off. About a mile up the road, I caught sight of the little shit, and he was holding Mum's purse.

"Okay," I said to the couple who had kindly stopped to give me a lift, "slow down. Thanks very much. Drop me here." They looked at each other, and the driver pulled over. The look on their faces was hysterical, but I was in no mood for a laugh. I jumped out while the car was still rolling, and he floored it like they had just escaped a kidnapping.

I tried to not look in the thief's direction, hoping he wouldn't notice me, and sure enough, the pretend gangster walked bang in front me. There he was, about to get a big slap. The look on his face was like "WTF! Where did you come from?" He threw Mum's purse on the ground and bolted. I picked up the purse and ran after him. He was fast off the mark, but I noticed he was slowing down very quickly. I had to stop myself from laughing. His jeans were ten sizes too big, and they were halfway down his bum, he had no belt, and his underpants were hanging out. He was trying to run whilst holding his pants up. I can tell you, it looked difficult, and he didn't get far.

He heard me breathing down his neck and stopped running. We were in the middle of the park, which was packed with couples and families picnicking. He spun around and caught me off guard when he pulled out a large pair of scissors and started making jabbing motions in my direction. I presumed he had used the scissors to break the locks on Mum's car. Anyway, that really pissed me off. I ignored the scissors and attacked viciously, in a flurry of punches to the head. He went down, dropped the scissors, and I sat on him until the police arrived with a canine (some people call them dogs).

The police let me know they had three witnesses who wanted me charged with assault. All they had seen was a crazy man beating the crap out of someone. The police were surprisingly relaxed and cool about everything. It turned out the guy was a known car thief and house breaker. I didn't tell the cops about the scissor attack because the guy was almost in tears and he looked a bit down, sitting in the back of the patrol car in handcuffs. Having said that, though, he did ask the police to charge me with assault. The policeman looked at me, rolled his eyes, stuck his head in the car, and said, "No chance."

I kept the drugs I found in his pocket, as part payment for breaking Mum's car and threatening to stab me, but also because he tried to sound like an American gangster, which he was not. I was late to the movie, and I had another broken finger, but what the heck.

I was now busy looking after a toddler and running two restaurants, when I realised that one of the managers and two of the chefs, who were brothers, were stealing money and stock. I put a stop to it by making sure they were caught red-handed. It was stressful and it took a few months to know exactly who was doing what and when. The night I confronted the head chef, it turned violent, and I killed him with a mallet. I cut him into little pieces, put him in a food processor and made dumplings. They were very tasty, actually, and they sold extremely well. They were profitable too; on account of the fact he was a fat bastard. However, I did feel a tad guilty when his pregnant wife rang and said he hadn't come home.

Just kidding, I haven't murdered anyone. Well, not yet. Keep reading, though!

Kylea had been learning Middle Eastern dance for years and had developed into an excellent dancer with a brilliant reputation. Kylea's mum had been a dance teacher and Kylea had found her vocation. She started teaching and performing on a regular basis, including traveling interstate, which meant Grace literally came with me everywhere. Luckily for me, she was easy to look after. We put a lot of work into those businesses for a few more years, then sold and moved down south again, right in front of a beautiful surf beach. Grace was about three years old when we bought a large café. We renovated it and turned it into a good business.

Meanwhile, I was still seeing my doctor in the city every ten or twelve weeks, to get scripts. Around this time, I injured my back with a bulging disc, which is painful. The best treatment for a bulging disc, however, is exercise like walking and swimming. When my doctor saw the x-ray, he said he had an opportunity to register with the Medical Board for chronic back pain. I didn't understand at the time why this was necessary, as I wasn't in chronic pain. He didn't discuss it with me; he just told me what he was doing. My relationship with him was deteriorating and for some time it had started to resemble that of a dealer and an addict. Within a few weeks my back was better, and yet I was now registered with the Medical Board as needing Subutex for chronic pain, and I would find out later, on a permanent basis! This was confirmed years later by a psychiatrist at DASA, as she sat holding my medical records. She said that my GP was effectively lying to the Medical Board and, in her words, "fudging the books"!

This explains why each time I went to see other doctors for help, or even to ask advice about the best way to get off medication, my doctor would be notified and become angry with me. On many occasions, when I tried to explain that all I wanted to do was be free from medication, he would shut me down and say I was a "lifer." His mantra was a simple one. If I really wanted to stop, I could, and it was easy because it was all in my mind. He told me it would be akin to him taking three or four Panadeine Forte for a few days and stopping. It was an absurd remark. He wasn't listening to anything I had to say. He knew I had chronic insomnia and cutting the medication back just a minuscule amount exacerbated the problem. It was not manageable, and suffering every day wears you down. He would just look at me, ignore my concerns, and tap his head whilst saying it was all in my mind. His answer was to put me on antidepressants. I felt I had no option other than to ignore the side-effects and the frustration. I took the antidepressants. I should have thrown them in the bin where they belonged.

The café was super busy, Grace would come to work with me all day and socialise with the customers, usually the adults; and, I might add, help herself to their food, drinks, and anything else she fancied. Kylea was dancing professionally and organising shows, festivals, and events. And after almost ten years, I was back into music, and I put together a band called The Fyoogs.

We moved further south and into a little house in a holiday park with a pool, a back garden made up of sand dunes, the beach and bush. Kylea got pregnant again with Ava and I trotted off to get a vasectomy. Of course, that had to go horribly wrong didn't it, with internal bleeding or something. No matter, it was only my BALLS! They became so swollen and purple they literally looked like two giant fucking eggplants. I couldn't stand, sit, or even lie down without pain. I went back to hospital and saw the surgeon. He walked into the room, had a quick look, and ran out again. "Shit that's not good." He returned soon after with eight or nine students in tow. I was just thinking this couldn't get any more embarrassing, when without any warning he threw the covers off, leaving me there completely naked with two eggplants where my balls used to be. The room went deathly quiet, the surgeon cleared his throat and said, rather loudly and, I might add, with a weird sense of pride, "Spectacular!"

Things did return to normal after a few anxious weeks, and I can vividly remember the first test run. My eyes watered!

Back at the café one day, I had a visit from four police officers who said they wanted to buy the business. I said no but changed my mind when they showed me their plans. They described starting up a very similar business in the same area, and they had a million dollars to invest, or so they said. They were adamant that it was either sell up or someone was going to go broke. I sold up! We took time off, to do nothing other than what we wanted, which for me was music. I started jamming around with different people again, buying better instruments and equipment and writing songs. Writing music has always come easily and naturally; it's the lyrics that take a little longer.

Ava's birth was a different experience. In fact, it was a nightmare of epic proportions. Firstly, the labour went on for what seemed like days, and I was running out of movies to watch. Then the midwife went into a panic and said Ava was stuck and the wrong way around. They rushed Kylea off to have a cesarean, but as we went into the operating room, I told them that Kylea didn't want a cesarean. What I should have said is, please don't operate unless it is an emergency. I didn't realise Ava's heart had stopped beating. Things became chaotic very quickly, and I knew Kylea and Ava were in trouble. Without a word, there were at least a dozen people in the room. I was filled with a sense of dread. I felt completely useless. I was asked to get out of the way and stand back. I couldn't even try and reassure Kylea.

After a harrowing few minutes, they somehow managed to eventually pull Ava out by her arm. Immediately, two doctors started working on her, trying to get her heart going and start her breathing. Meanwhile, some other doctors tried to stop Kylea from bleeding to death, it was that bad! I was stuck in the middle of Ava and Kylea, and I couldn't help. I stood at the back of the room and let the tears roll down my face. After a minute or so, Ava's heart started, and they got her breathing.

Ava was moved to another room and put in a small perspex box where they could monitor her. I went with Ava, held her tiny little hand, and prayed she would pull through. As soon as she started to improve, I went to look for Kylea and I found her in a small side room, on her own and lying in a pool of blood, shaking. She was still bleeding heavily, so I kicked up a real stink, got some help and Kylea slowly recovered. I let a sense of relief wash over me, and suddenly I was completely exhausted. I can't imagine how Kylea felt. She was white as a ghost and looked absolutely shattered. Welcome to the world, Ava! You will always be loved, but you will need to be brave and strong.

I'll be there

Through wind and rain

Fall with you to keep you safe

Until your time to fly away

I'll be there most everyday

God, when I heard the word,

Touched my very heart

Pulled me into line and

Freed me from the past

Hasten forth

With a will of steel

Resolute and strong

Knowing in life's long dream

The treasure is a song.

Chapter Sixteen

WHATEVER IT TAKES

A man's life can only be determined by
what he does, not what he says

My struggle with medication was getting worse and becoming more difficult to manage, partly, I presume, because of my age, and partly because of the length of time I had been taking it. My body was starting to react to the side-effects more aggressively. I remember that when I first raised concerns with my doctor about taking Subutex long-term, he laughed it off and said, "Think yourself lucky you won't be feeling all the little aches and pains the rest of us have to put up with." I know that after just a few years, I was dealing with constant and chronic pain in my knees, elbows, ankles, and feet. I used to lie in bed and feel a deep, throbbing pain radiating from my whole body. I had also developed a nasty and painful stomach ulcer that, despite an endoscopy and treatment, persisted. I hadn't consumed alcohol for over two decades, but I found it very difficult quitting cigarettes. Taking Subutex at 5am was not a healthy way to start the day. I would wake up feeling as if I had taken amphetamines, so I would drink coffee, smoke cigarettes, and eat later.

I started a catering business part-time, just to make enough to pay the bills, and I would spend the rest of the time looking after and playing with the girls. Any spare time I had was put into music, writing songs, jamming, recording, putting bands together and playing gigs. I was still not making any real money performing, despite the hours of practice and band rehearsals. In fact, I was making less money than ever before, maybe just enough to cover costs.

I remember reading a quote from Iggy Pop: "Play hard, and don't expect to get paid." What a cunt! Easy to say when you're a rich bastard. What did Iggy do? He took his shirt off and jumped around the stage, acting like fucking Gollum! Seriously though, your doubts become louder. Maybe I am just not quite good enough! That maybe becomes probably, probably becomes certainly, and certainly becomes... bugger! OR:

Success is just the progressive realisation of a worthy ideal.

- Earl Nightingale

That still doesn't bring home the bacon, though, does it?

I heard from an old friend that there were rumours I was down and out, living in an old caravan, just like "them there trailer trash"!

Well, they were nearly right. I wasn't about to become Australian of the Year. It was true that we had no money, virtually no possessions, and a $500 car. But, no matter what, we were a family, we loved each other, the girls were thriving, and we were okay. As far as my family was concerned, I had been lucky, but you never know what's lurking around the corner.

When Ava was two, she caught whooping cough, and one night she collapsed in front of me, fell unconscious, and stopped breathing. I saw her go down and within three seconds, I was phoning an ambulance. Kylea picked Ava up, but she was like a rag doll and totally unresponsive. I was begging the operator to hurry up and opened the front door to look for the ambulance. As I did, a strong, cold wind blew into the house. We were in the middle of a winter storm, thank God. As soon as the cold hit Ava, she started breathing and regained consciousness. She went to hospital in the ambulance with her mum and I followed in the car. Ava recovered, but only for it to happen again.

This time, we rushed her to emergency ourselves and I got stuck behind an old man and his fifteen-year-old son. I had a real emergency, with a two-and-a-half-year-old who needed urgent medical attention. I became angry when I overheard the dad in front of me explaining to a doctor that a month ago his son had banged his elbow on a coffee table. I could see the staff were busy doing a difficult job and were getting frustrated with the man and his son, who did NOT have an emergency. I walked up to the boy, tapped him on the shoulder, and said, "Excuse me." I grabbed him by the scruff of the neck, and with all my might, ripped his arm off at the shoulder and shoved it up his arse. He was bleeding heavily, so I laid him on the ground, face down, on account of his arm being in the way. I leant over and politely asked him if he was a bit sore.

I was daydreaming again.

Ava had developed pneumonia, so she and her mum stayed a few days. The level of care at Flinders Hospital was excellent and, with her mum by her side, Ava made a full recovery. I can take almost any amount of physical pain, but not so good with emotional pain, especially something as unbearable as losing a child, anything but that!

Kylea went back to her dance and teaching. I was spending a lot of time on music, gigging, writing, and recording, but I also spent as much time with the girls as possible. I tried to become a better man and practised patience, love and understanding; well, when I wasn't losing my shit. When Grace was born, I made a promise with myself that no matter what the circumstances, I would never leave my family or take them for granted.

For a big part of my life, I had been reckless and irresponsible, and that would be on a good day when I was sober. I had been aggressive at times whilst abusing drugs and alcohol. I also mistreated and/or took advantage of some girlfriends, something I deeply regret. It took me a long time to admit that. I had always buried pain and it would gnaw away at me from the inside out. On occasion it would rear its ugly head and I would take it out on the people around me. Psychologists call it projection! One of my favorite poems is "A Poison Tree" by the genius, William Blake. I can appreciate that almost everyone gets a head fuck of one kind or another, but it is how you deal with it that really counts.

A POISON TREE

I was angry with my friend
I told my wrath; my wrath did end.
I was angry with my foe
I told it not, my wrath did grow.

And I water'd it in fears,
Night and morning with my tears
And I sunned it with smiles,
And with soft deceitful wiles.

And it grew both day and night,
Till it bore an apple bright
And my foe beheld it shine,
And he knew that it was mine,

And into my garden stole
When the night had veil'd the pole
In the morning glad I see
My foe outstretch'd beneath the tree.

WILLIAM BLAKE
(1757 - 1827)

One Of a Kind

Sitting on a mountain
With a flower in my hand
Loving every moment
Thought I was a man
Dancing in the moonlight
With the shadows of my soul
I thought I found reality
But I fell into a hole

Talk to the animals
Walk across the sea
Cry unto the sky
Fly into the breeze
Cutting up the waves
I am you and free
Breaking down the doors
As far as you can see.

Chapter Seventeen

THE DEEPER THE SORROW, THE GREATER THE JOY

We are the music makers and dreamers of dreams

Jump forward a few years, and music is still my love and passion. Adelaide is relatively small, and by the early 2000s, the whole scene was a shadow of its former self. The introduction of pokie machines in all the pubs instigated the decline of what was, in the '70s, '80s and '90s, a robust and healthy live music scene, punching way above its weight nationally. More recently, the problem became the internet, and a generation of young people who were generally not that interested in going out at all. The festivals were booming for a few years, but even they are in decline.

I could still get a few people together to jam, and I was writing songs profusely, which meant I was back in the studio. I had started recording in the eighties with Stuart of Artec, Triple M radio and Triple J. The mid Nineties, I was recording again at mix masters with Stuart and then Mick. Ten years later, I formed "The Fyoogs" and recorded a few EPs, albums, and singles with Evan at Broadcast which had a great set-up and vibe. That closed in about 2010. After that, I did a few sessions with Dave at AGS; and a little later released an album called "Oceans," with good friend, Matt; and then onto Twin Earth with Jono, where I still record to this day.

February 2022, I have just released another album called Dust, recorded and produced by Evan.

Across The Sea

I'm in the silence
Sorrow everywhere
Here in the sands of time
Feel it in the air
When you come to find me
Reach across the sea
There on the island
Of forgotten memories

I found her there
Rest her soul in my hands
Lay her down to rest
Gently in the sand
Here we go on a hot summer breeze
Looking for an island
There across the sea

Burning in the fire
Trapped here in a dream
Taking forever
Who I want to be
I know something's
Playing with my life
I'll tread carefully
The devil I need to fight

There I was dreaming
Tales of Odyssey
Let it all go now
I'm running free
Let the night fall
The sun can reach the sky
Evading shadows
In the darkness of my mind

Chapter Eighteen

MEDITATIONS ON HELL

The sky lies open

I think just about every adult on the planet will remember 2020. I certainly will, but it will be for a different reason than most. I was turning fifty-seven in February, and I was still primarily focused on music. For the last few years, because I couldn't make a living from music, I had been doing any kind of work I could get, and that usually meant manual labour. When you do a day's hard yakka, it becomes a challenge to make time for anything else, let alone getting out to band rehearsals. That's how it is if you love something, though, you find a way.

I contacted DASA, a drug and alcohol recovery service, and asked to be admitted to their detox facility in the city. I could not go on taking medication. I had been on drugs for forty-two years. The last twenty years had been strictly on doctor's orders with no drugs other than what was prescribed and no alcohol. However, the last nineteen years had strangely been the most difficult. I was obviously older, but I believe I had been on prescription medication, including antidepressants, for way longer than I ever needed to be. However, I couldn't stop without help, mainly because I would suffer from akathisia and a severe form of insomnia.

The side-effects of taking prescription drugs for nineteen years were having a devastating effect on my physical and mental health. My liver was in a bad way, with one doctor telling me I had just a few years left before I would need a transplant or die. It had caused severe osteoporosis, and although Subutex can be prescribed for pain management, it was paradoxically causing me constant pain. It was debilitating, exhausting, and my doctor was still fobbing me off and persisting with the ludicrous idea that it was simply mind over matter.

There were several complex issues that he would not consider, or dismissed outright. In the very early mornings, as the opiates in my brain wore off, I would often suffer from horrific nightmares. This might not sound like a big deal, but after decades it becomes difficult to maintain a healthy, balanced mental state. As the years wore on, it was becoming increasingly difficult to function normally. I was taking this stuff every day for almost twenty years, and it was a daily rollercoaster ride of ups and downs. One minute it would affect me like amphetamines, and an hour later I would be zonked out. An hour later and I could be dealing with anxiety and severe stomach cramps. I hadn't slept properly in almost thirty years, and I was mentally and physically drained.

I went to see my doctor for the last time in early February 2020 and told him I wanted to detox with DASA and that I would need a referral. He REFUSED, insisting I should relax and let him manage it. He wrote me a script for some patches, but it was exactly the same drug. I had followed his directions and taken his medications for twenty years without putting a foot wrong. Yet he refused to write me a referral to a specialised detox facility. I think my doctor was caught in a lie that he had created about eighteen years earlier when he had written to the Medical Board. The reason he gave the Medical Board, in asking for permission to prescribe me Subutex, was chronic back pain. I'm not sure why he would lie. Maybe it was just easier and less complicated. I don't know.

I went back to the nurse at the detox center and explained the situation, and after a few days, she rang and told me I would be admitted without a referral. I now had a few days to prepare myself for another trip to hell! I had a pretty good idea of what to expect. I wouldn't need to pack much, that's for sure. I took a toothbrush.

Kylea dropped me at the detox centre and I hugged her for a long time, secretly harbouring second thoughts. I said a very apprehensive goodbye and watched her walk away. I went in, ready to face the music. I was met by a male nurse. We filled in the paperwork and got buzzed through security and the many locked doors. I was shown to my room, which consisted of a bed, sink, shower, and toilet, pretty much like my prison cell in the army. Beggars can't be choosers. The nurse searched me and my bag. No belongings allowed, including phones. The security people showed me into a treatment room, and I met the psychiatrist. As soon as I sat down, an alarm sounded, which created quite a stir, and the psychiatrist ran out of the room. She returned about ten minutes later, looking a bit agitated. I found out later that someone had been stashing their medication and taken it all at once in a suicide attempt.

We started the interview again and she immediately noticed what she thought was an error in my medical records which, of course, by now were the size of an old phone book. She looked a bit concerned and said that according to my records I was being prescribed the drug Subutex for chronic back pain!

The psychiatrist looked extremely uncomfortable. She said, "Your doctor, Simon, is part of the fraternity here at the hospital, so I have to be careful. But he has fudged the books, and I will not be doing the same."

Many years earlier, I was interviewed by a researcher from Flinders University, who told me that she had never heard of anyone being on Subutex for as long as I had, and that in fact she had not heard of anyone being prescribed Subutex long-term at all!

The psychiatrist looked flustered, got up, and said she was going to discuss my case with another psychiatrist. After about twenty minutes, she returned and said, "Look, Simon, this drug you have been on for nineteen years is supposed to be used for a maximum of six weeks. In fact, we don't use it at all. We haven't for a long time. It's nasty, very hard to get off, and there are better options." She sat looking at me, as if expecting some sort of explanation.

I didn't know what to say at first, then I spoke as follows. "Look, I'm sorry, I have been following my doctor's instructions for the last nineteen years. I have tried many times to reduce, cut back and stop, but the main obstacle, as I kept telling my doctor, was being unable to sleep, often for days and even weeks. I have tried many, many times over the years and I have been asking my doctor for help for over fifteen years."

There was a stunned silence and an awkward moment, while she looked through my medical records again.

"Well, I can give you something to help you sleep while you are here, but I suggest you stay on the antidepressants and focus on getting off the Subutex. You can have this nicotine pipe replaced every few hours." She handed me a small plastic pipe.

"No, if I'm here and I'm going through hell, I want to quit smoking and quit the antidepressants as well. I want my life back."

She raised her eyebrows, pulled a face and said, "I don't recommend it, but okay. Good luck, Simon."

There was a very telling incident just a few years ago. I received a phone call from my doctor. He was very angry, and he was shouting, "Simon, what do you think you're doing?"

"What do you mean? I'm sorry, I don't understand."

"I think you do. You saw a doctor yesterday and complained about the care you are getting."

"No, I did not."

"Well, it sounded like you were complaining. Don't you dare talk to anyone about your treatment and medication."

I was a bit shocked, and said, "I'm sorry. It's a misunderstanding. I was just there to get a referral for carpal tunnel, and the doctor asked me why I was on Subutex."

He calmed down, but as usual finished with the last word. "Don't let it happen again."

I was frustrated, but at the same time I had to be careful. He had the upper hand. I was still dependent on him. The reason that phone call was relevant is that, as I have recently learnt, it was immediately after he had been dragged in front of the health practices tribunal and found guilty of professional misconduct over the death of one of his patients. This was obviously the reason he was so angry. He saw me as a potential problem.

Back in the room at DASA, a nurse came in and went through all the medical protocols, tests, and information. I didn't pay much notice to what she said, as I had already started to come down horribly. I didn't care. I went to my room and waited.

It's a hellish trip and probably unique to everyone. I can't imagine anybody I love or care about going through it, and if possible, I would swap places with them in a heartbeat. I couldn't bear not to; it really is that terrifying. It's like something from a horror movie; there's no escape and nothing to do except try to hang on. You can get really tested when the hallucinations start. It's a long, terrifying descent into the depths of hell.

I talked to myself a lot, as though I had become my best friend. I had to keep reassuring myself that the demons were not real, and this ride would end eventually, if only I could hang on. I remember thinking of Kylea, Grace and Ava. They were a big part of the reason I wanted to break free. That and trying to retain what little self-respect I had left. At least Django was with me.

"Who is Django?" I hear you ask.

Django is part of the family and a Zen master. Some might say he is just a cat. I thought he was with me all week, but I am told he was at home, looking after the girls. However, there is a possibility that he's like one of those subatomic particles that can be in two places at the same time. Despite being at home, he was with me, and I was talking to him for my entire stay. We even communicated telepathically. I remember always having to make room for him on the bed. Well actually, it was more him leaving a little spot for me; but he was great company, and I needed a friend.

That first night, I had all the usual symptoms associated with severe withdrawals: nausea, vomiting, diarrhoea, shaking, fever, sweats, stomach cramps, extreme anxiety, hallucinations, and difficulty breathing. In other words, it was a bit like a family Christmas! Probably the hardest symptom to deal with, however, was akathisia. I had it terribly, especially in my legs, and I had no control over it. After a prolonged period, it can induce psychosis. I remember bashing my head against the wall so hard one night that I broke a tooth in half and knocked another one out. I couldn't think rationally and thought that perhaps I could get into trouble with the staff. I threw the tooth down the toilet.

Trying to describe the mental torture, rather than the physical stuff, is a lot more difficult. I remember Dad, when I was in the throes of withdrawals, asking me what it was like. He kept saying, "You look all right, Si. Why not just sit it out?"

"Dad, if only it was that easy! I wish I could. You don't understand, you can't understand. I'm too sick to explain, Dad. Can I borrow some money and then I'll get to the doctor's?"

"Well, try to explain to me how you're feeling. You don't look too bad."

"Dad, I don't look that sick yet, because it's only just started. In a couple of hours, I'll be climbing the walls." He gave me the money and I ran! I am sorry, Dad.

It reminded me of the time as a teenager when I went to stay for a few days with him in Sydney. He took me out in his boat on the river, dropped anchor and said, "So, Si, tell me about yourself." Jesus Christ, I wanted to jump in the water and swim back. But I couldn't, because there were bull sharks.

Trying to describe how you feel when you suddenly stop heroin, methadone, Subutex and antidepressants, well, it's a bit like trying to describe a beautifully stunning sunset, or a bizarre dream. You can try, but words will never suffice. Nothing you could say would even come close.

I can try, though, can't I?

Imagine suffering from extreme food poisoning. Okay, now imagine you have been buried alive; you have lost control of your body; throw in a shit load of anxiety and claustro-phobia. Okay, well done. Now imagine dealing with that for a week, or at least a few days and nights, and no sleeping. Hope-fully you have a good imagination. I am starting to suspect a lot of people don't - not you, of course, seeing as you're reading my book and all.

For the whole time I was there I can only remember eating one tub of yogurt. The smell of food made me feel sick. I can't remember even drinking any water. I lost ten kilos and it wasn't as if I was overweight when I went in. After a few days, I started to come out of my room for a few minutes at a time and going into a communal area. The first person I met was a young overweight man with incredibly flabby arms. He just looked at me and said, "I've been in here fourteen times." He was an alcoholic. Really, the place had no standards!

I felt terribly sorry for the guy. He looked at home, and it made me sad. I had forgotten that getting through detox is just a small part of the recovery process. Once you're out of hospital, you're on your own, and there is not a lot of support or sympathy for drug addicts and alcoholics. Funny about that! One of the first things I noticed was that about eighty percent of the people in there were young women. Drugs and alcohol can really fuck you up, no matter who you are. Seeing the young women there made me even more determined to make a full recovery. That would be the only way I could have an honest conversation with my daughters about the real and ever-present danger of addiction.

Most of the patients were having daily group therapy sessions. I didn't attend them, and I avoided talking to anyone as much as possible, except Django, of course. I was in too much pain, and I knew what I had to do: get clean and get out. I asked the psychiatrist if I could leave. She recommended I stay, but I was adamant. I needed to be home by the sea. It was late summer, and I knew I would feel better if I could get in the ocean. I always had.

Kylea picked me up the next day, and after going through security, I stepped outside and breathed in the fresh air. God, I felt sick!

It was more than comforting to get a hug, and I needed all the help I could get. What a difference a smile and a hug can make! I stopped in the garden near the car and tried to gather my thoughts and remember what it was like to be human. It took some time for my eyes to adjust to the light, and after a moment, I noticed the movement of the wind in the trees and the smell of fresh air and the scent of eucalyptus. What I experienced visually appeared strange, powerful, and beautiful at the same time. Everything seemed to move in unison. I had a strong feeling everything was as it should be. Then I looked up and noticed the intense, radiant blue of the sky. It was breathtaking. I felt calm and stood still, taking in the green of the grass and the colour of the plants and flowers. It felt as if I had stepped into another world. It was a profound experience. I had taken everything for granted. I was a wreck, but at least now I was on the right path. I was heading home, and the ocean called.

Who Turned Out the Lights?

You know it's time to make things right
Do it now, changing your mind
Eat the dark, drinking the light
Find your soul in the middle of the night
Descend the tree when the darkness comes
Across the sea and into the sun

Tear it down, stand up and fight. Can you tell me
Who turned out the light?

You've seen it now, you've seen the light
We call it hope that makes us feel alive
Where you stand reaching for stars
Unlock the key that leads to your heart
Gentle waves of give and take
Steppingstones lie in your wake
Here we are, dancing in the light
The sun of God is just a fire in the sky

Tear it down, stand up and fight. Can you tell me
Who turned out the light?

The stream of life
Running through your veins
The power of the sun in your heart and in your brain
Hope's the flame creating the light that we all need
To make us feel alive
Different faces in oceans of time
Different places, makes you feel fine
Here we are, dancing in the light
The sun of God is just a fire in the sky.

Chapter Nineteen

I SWIM BECAUSE I CAN'T FLY

Remember you are of noble birth
You carry the essence of God within you

March 2020.

The moment I arrived home, I staggered down the beach and fell into the ocean. The water was calm, clear, clean, and autumn cool. I swam out into the Gulf as far as I could, until I reached the point of exhaustion. Treading water, I turned to face the shoreline and I could just make out the beach.

Maybe I should just keep going!

I was thinking about the long road ahead. I was tired of all the suffering. I wanted my life back, but the question was, did I have the energy, courage, and determination? Was I too late? I thought of the girls at home with Kylea and knew, I didn't have a choice. I turned back and started a difficult, slow swim, all the way until at last I could lie on my back in the shallows. I was exhausted, but I mustered enough energy to walk home through the sand dunes. I look back now and realise that all I had done was detox. I hadn't even started to recover. In fact, I was completely spaced out. My brain was damaged, and it was going to take a very long time to recover. It was just the beginning. I had a long road ahead, and it was going to be getting dark.

I was still suffering badly from withdrawals. I had developed blurred vision, which cannot be treated or improved by wearing glasses. It is my brain and not my eyes. I just hope that it will improve with time. However, the main problem, which had plagued me on and off for decades and had resurfaced with a vengeance, was chronic insomnia and akathisia. I tried everything except taking more damn pills, but nothing worked. I focused on diet, exercise, and meditation.

One morning, about a week or so after hospital, I hadn't slept at all, not even for a few minutes. I had gone for a walk in the early hours of the morning and started hallucinating. I saw little demons appear, hovering over my shoulder, and it was frightening. I had taken LSD and magic mushrooms hundreds of times, and although it was a long time ago, I remembered how to stay in control and remain calm. I had talked myself through bad trips before, and I could do it again. It was an exhausting ordeal, though, and I was only just hanging on. I started talking to the little demon faces as I walked through the bush.

"*I gotta sleep. Are you gunna help?*" Really, it was just me and the kangaroos. "*Come on, I gotta sleep, I gotta sleep, why's it so hard to sleep? I'd do anything for a few minutes sleep, I could* slip into the abyss, shit what's that? Who are you? What do you want?" Little black faces and shapes appeared, flicking and dancing around my left shoulder. They kept changing shape and getting in my face.

"Go away. You don't scare me. I've had too much practice at this, so fuck off and leave me alone."

I climbed up one of the sand dunes and sat down. I closed my eyes, and waited for sunrise.

I woke Kylea early and told her I was going to emergency at one of the big hospitals. Thankfully, she insisted on coming with me. We waited a couple of hours until a doctor came in to see me. He literally looked about twenty years old, and of course, he went through all the protocols and a big explanation of why he could not prescribe anything to help me sleep. His hands were tied.

I had tears rolling down my cheeks. I was just holding it together and had barely slept a few hours in more than a week. Now, desperate people do desperate things, and I couldn't go home. The psychosis had started. I mentioned to him that I might just go up to the roof! I just needed to sleep. He threatened to admit me into a mental health ward, against my will. I didn't like the sound of that. I'd only just got out of one hospital and I wasn't going to another. I got up to leave, and as I did, a nurse from DASA walked into the room and said she could help. What a godsend. She saved my life that day, and I don't even remember her name. She interviewed me for about an hour, made some calls and got a psychiatrist to write me a small script over the phone. Kylea drove me home. I took a sleeping pill and went to bed.

Chronic lack of sleep is torture, quite literally. It's cruel and inhumane, and after a few days without any sleep there is a breaking point. I had a week's supply of sleeping tablets. I broke the tablets in half and only took them as a last resort. My mum and dad both used sleeping tablets and it has been linked with dementia. Dad died from dementia a few years ago and Mum is in the early stages. It's an insidious disease.

What really kept me awake at night however was akathisia. I looked it up, talked to doctors, and read whatever I could find. I bought supplements and exercised, walking on the beach, taking small runs through the sand dunes, and of course swimming, all of which sounds very straightforward, but if you're not sleeping and suffering from withdrawals it can be very challenging. Every morning I would wake with nausea and a very strange, awful pain in the base of my head, like pins and needles, but in the brain. I was still getting brain zaps, which can occur when coming off antidepressants suddenly. The psychologist I was speaking to told me the brain can't feel pain, and ordinarily I would agree. But I had experienced excruciating pain when taking the Naltrexone, and now that I'd stopped the Subutex and antidepressants, I was experiencing a horrible brain pain. It was not a headache and yes, I know it rhymes rather nicely.

Kylea's brother Tim put me onto the Ice Man, aka, Wim Hoff. He has a brilliant yet simple method of breath work and cold- water therapy which I believe has helped enormously, and I have stuck with it every day religiously. The winter swims are hard work and painfully cold, especially on your head. It may take about five or ten minutes, but eventually your body adjusts. Strangely, it is the only time I feel almost human.

At first, I thought I could recover in a few months. I soon changed that to six months, and then I had the goal to be better by the time Grace's 18th birthday arrived. That's been and gone a year and a half ago, so now I am trying to be more realistic yet hopeful. The doctor I see now is a younger man. A couple of doctors have admitted to me that the medical profession don't fully understand how some drugs work, including anti-depressants, let alone what happens to the brain with long term-use, or when you stop taking the medication!

I have done all I can to make my recovery as swift as possible. There is something else I do which has helped, and that is playing, writing, and listening to music. When I left the detox centre, just about any good music I heard had a profound effect on me. For a while at least, my world seemed so terribly sad.

Apart from my vision, which is chronically blurred, my senses now seem to be highlighted. I think that all drugs do in the end is dumb you down, deaden the senses and turn everything into mediocrity. Although I am far from recovered, when I play music now, I feel a lot more. It's hard to explain, but music has taken on a greater importance, and I couldn't live without it. It speaks to me more beautifully and it has given my life meaning. The same can be said for poetry, which can be incredibly powerful and inspiring.

A few years ago, we had a fire that started in the garage and destroyed all my studio recordings. I also lost the old surfing films that friends had taken over the years, as well as photos, and I even lost my surfboards. The fire spread into the house, and we lost a lot of stuff. Our landlords were insured but we were not. A few days after the fire a CSI officer came over to establish how the fire had started, and although I already knew, I was saying nothing. The landlord wanted a big juicy pay-out, not the facts.

The garage had been incinerated. It had been an intense fire fanned by very strong winds from a storm. The CSI officer let his imagination go wild and went through his version with me in graphic detail. He explained how the wind had blown a hanging light down, which had then smashed onto some damaged electrical wiring, and this caused a spark and set fire to some old books. I duly congratulated him on his powers of deduction, whilst I looked around for Dr Watson and wondered why he wasn't wearing a funny hat! I didn't mention it at the time, but there was no light in the garage and the electricity had been cut off years ago. I think he wanted to sign off and go home. At any rate, I lost decades of work. All my recordings that went back to the beginning were incinerated.

I have met some new musicians recently and have started on another album. In this book I have included some poems, quotes, and song lyrics. However, all my writing is simply about life lessons I need to learn, accept, and act upon. Walk the talk, so to speak. It's all the stuff I need to hear and probably always will.

Pleasures of Illusion

I want to run with you
Toward the stars
Sure there's a path
A light in the dark

Does the light
Occupy your side
Nothings free
Walk with me

Here we are
Lighting up the dark
Toward the stars
Not without you

Throw your arms
Around the sun
Oceans in your eye
Pale by the mountainside

Open your heart
Welcome the rain
Like the sand
Washed away

Lift my soul
With open arms
Embrace the path
Let her go

See the ocean

Hear the wind

Feel the sand

Upon your skin

Taste the water

She'll let you in

The raven flies

With open wings

Chapter Twenty

UNDER THE HEAL OF DESTINY

Today is the only day where we can create a better future

Dr Gabor Mate, who is a world-renowned, highly respected addiction expert, speaker, and bestselling author, suggests that addiction is not a choice, it is not a moral failure, it is not an ethical lapse, it is not a weakness of character, it is not a failure of will, which is how society depicts addiction. It is not an inherited brain disease, which is how the medical community tend to see it. But it is actually a response to human suffering, and that is what the scientific and research literature shows. It is an attempt to escape suffering temporarily. The problem is having deep emotional pain or problems you didn't know what to do with. So, the question becomes: *Why did you lack the internal resources to deal with that pain in a more creative, forward-looking way that would help resolve the pain, rather than perpetuate it?*

It's been two years and I have improved, although sometimes it doesn't feel like it. My vision is still blurred, I have difficulty sleeping, and I have other complications from long-term medication. I have kept to a routine and every day I grit my teeth and get on with it, as most good people do. I hope to keep improving, especially my eyesight and energy levels. Who knows? The doctors, psychiatrists and psychologists certainly don't know. Meanwhile I hope to keep writing, playing, recording, jamming, and performing with some great musicians and friends.

I stayed under the care of my doctor for twenty-five years. I have not heard from him since detoxing, and I never will. It was my wife and children along with the ocean, music, and friends, that saved my life.

Although I obviously have many regrets, I am also eternally grateful and owe so much to so many. I have been fortunate enough to meet hundreds of great people who have been incredibly honest, kind, supportive, patient and loving. I hope that one day they may know how much I appreciated, and in some cases still appreciate, their company, knowledge, love, and friendship.

My focus is as strong as ever and my goals are clear.

No matter what it takes I will look after my family, meditate, breathe, swim, play, and dream of a future free of addiction, but filled with hard work, music, challenges, adventure, love, learning and friendship ... or maybe at least try and keep my room tidy!

Don't be afraid to step into the dark

Keep walking, following the stars

Face your death, along the road

Embrace the path you walk alone

You can find another world
Where the ocean meets the sky
The paradise you feign to seek
Is lost within your mind

Still the waters
Should they reflect
Deep within your eye
I heard the children sing just now
Move stars around the sky

The cold ghost moon
That falls tonight
Will leave another day
Now you can grasp the silence
On any winters day

Here we are
I don't know why
Illusion is just fine
Though shifting sands and false of mind
Fall through space and time

The lonely sea that sings for me
Like diamonds in thine eye
Shows me of a way to be
In that earthly paradigm

TO CONTACT THE AUTHOR..

Thefyoogs@gmail.com

Drug and alcohol counselling service

Website: hartcentre.com

Email: info@hartcentre.com

Text: 0449898925

FOR MORE OF HARTLEY'S WORK...

"Whisky soaked vocals and a barrage of gritty riffs"

- DB Magazine.

Facebook:

Youtube:

Bandcamp:

APRIL 2022

Dust Album

Andrew Gaborit, drums and percussion.
Tasman Daish, piano, organ and synthesizer.
Mitchell Bedford, Bass guitar, editing, production
and arrangements.
Simon Hartley electric and acoustic guitars and vocals.
Paris Clark-proud, Acoustic rhythm guitar on "The Desert".
Recorded and produced by Evan James.
Recorded at Twin Earth recording studios, Adelaide.
All songs written by Simon Hartley.

ACKNOWLEDGEMENTS

I'd also like to thank all the community radio stations that support original music.

Thanks to Tim Bedford and Susie Raneskold for editing. Special thanks to Margie Gurner.

And finally thank you to my daughters Grace and Ava and my wife Kylea.

I would like to acknowledge the great bands of Adelaide and the Punters in the 80's and 90's that created such a vibrant, live music scene.

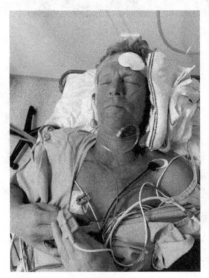

March 2022

Note to self- no more cliff jumping.